HOW TO
CLIMB
HARDER
Mark Reeves

First published 2010

Published in Great Britain 2010 by Pesda Press
Unit 22, Galeri
Doc Victoria
Caernarfon
Gwynedd
LL55 1SQ

ISBN: 978-1-906095-11-6

Printed and bound in Poland. www.polskabook.pl

Contents

THE AUTHOR 5
ACKNOWLEDGEMENTS 7
PARTICIPATION STATEMENT 8

How to Climb Harder — 9
LAZY CLIMBING 10

Learning — 11

Safety First — 15
RISK: TOP ROPING 16
EQUIPMENT CARE 41
RISK: LEAD CLIMBING 44
RISK: BOULDERING 52

Warming Up: Body & Mind — 57
STRETCHING 60
EXERCISE YOUR MIND 65

The Basics: Footwork & Balance — 67

The Basics: Handholds & Body Position — 75
CRIMPS 76
CUPPING 78
SLOPERS 79
PINCHES & SPRAGS 79
JAMMING 80
ORIENTATION 87
FLAGGING 89

Basic Hands-off Rests — 91
LEDGE REST 92
SLAB REST 92
CORNER REST 93
ARÊTE REST 95
CHIMNEY REST 96
ONE-FOOTED REST 97

Moving Up — 99
ROCK-OVERS 99
CORKSCREW ROCK-OVERS & THE RULE OF OPPOSITES 102

CORNERS 105
THE LAYBACK 106
THE MANTELSHELF 108
ARÊTES 110
CHIMNEYS 111
ROOFS 113
OVERHANGING WALLS 115

Advanced Technique & Bouldering 117

Putting It All Together 131

GUIDEBOOKS 132
READING ROUTES 134
STYLE OF ASCENT 136

Lead Climbing Techniques 139

CLIPPING QUICKDRAWS 139
ORGANISING YOUR RACK 143
WHAT'S IN YOUR RACK 144
PLACING GEAR EFFICIENTLY 153
RISKY LEADS 154
SINGLE VS DOUBLE ROPES 155

Mind Games 159

FEAR OF FALLING 174

Training: Basic Principles 175

THE WEAKEST LINK 176
GOAL SETTING 178
BASIC TRAINING 180

Training: Strength 185

GENERAL STRENGTH 186
SPECIFIC STRENGTH 186
MAXIMUM STRENGTH 195
EXPLOSIVE STRENGTH (POWER) 196

Training: Endurance 199

Training: Fitness 203

TRAINING: THE YOUNG CLIMBER 207

Nutrition 211

EATING DISORDERS & SPORT 218

Mark Reeves (self portrait) on top of
the First Flat Iron in Colorado, on the
outskirts of The City of Boulder, during
a three week tour climbing some of
the United States of America's classic
rock climbs. Managing to climb a
total of sixteen routes, eighty pitches
and covering over 2,000 miles.

You can keep up with Mark's latest
travels, climbs and coaching tips at
lifeinthevertical.com
Book the climbing course of a lifetime at
www.snowdoniamountainguides.com

THE AUTHOR

Mark Reeves

Mark has been a rock climbing instructor since
1997, working throughout the length and breadth
of North Wales. In 2005 Mark completed the
Mountain Instructor Award whilst working for
Plas y Brenin and has been a freelance/associ-
ate Instructor for them ever since. Mark has
sought to develop his coaching to the highest
level through various forms of Continuing
Professional Development, including BMC
Fundamentals and Learning to Train courses,
Plas y Brenin's Coaching Processes course and
finally completing an MSc in Applied Sports
Science at Bangor University.

This book brings together the academic, practical and personal skills he has developed over the
last thirteen years as a climber and coach; climbing routes of all different styles ranging from Diff
to E5 in over ten countries. In essence this book
is a shortcut to all Mark's accrued knowledge
over his long and successful professional and
personal climbing career.

The diagrams, photos and illustrations throughout the book are available to download as teaching resources for your own slideshow presentations.

visit: www.pesdapress.com/climbharder

ACKNOWLEDGEMENTS

This book was born out of a personal challenge to improve my own teaching and coaching as a mountaineering and climbing instructor. I have been guided and influenced by many coaches in many disciplines and walks of life. In particular working on the Instructor Scheme and subsequent years freelancing for Plas y Brenin, the National Mountain Centre, I have come under the stewardship of many highly qualified and experienced instructors who started me on the path which lead to this book. In particular I would like to extend my thanks to the following staff at the centre; Martin Chester, Pete Catterall, Loel Collins, Si Colley, Mike Raine, Jon 'Spike' Green, Dave Hollinger, Stu McAleese, Neil Johnson, Carlo Forte, Louise Turner and Pete Firth as well as others who are too numerous to mention. I have been given encouragement, inspiration and knowledge by all. Some of you may recognise some of your teaching methods in this book.

Conversations with other guides, instructors, teachers, coaches and climbers on the subject have shaped my thinking. They are also too numerous to mention, but Llion Morris, Liz Gunby, Libby Peters, Steve Mayers, Bryn Williams and Katherine Schumacher have been most influential.

Other influences have come from more mainstream sources like Dave Binney (BMC National Squad Coach) and his FUNdamentals Course and the BMC National Source Group for Coaching, which I have become involved with through BMC Cymru/Wales. I have sought to cover many of the areas that the United Kingdom Coaching Council recommend for their coaching schemes.

On top of the expertise of coaches and instructors many friends and acquaintances have helped me fashion these ideas into plain English. These people include Sonja Drummond, Helen Baker, Cheymoon O'Reilly, Rob Wilson and Sarah Clough.

Finally my thanks are extended to the staff at University of Wales, Bangor, who tutored me through the taught elements of an MSc in Applied Sports Science, in particular Mike Khan for his work of skill acquisition, Nicki Callow for sport psychology, Jamie MacDonald for the physiology and Ross Roberts for supervising my thesis on imagery and climbing.

There will be people that I have forgotten to thank and for this I apologise, although the last people I should acknowledge are Franco Ferrero for believing in the project and agreeing to publish this and Pete Wood for turning my scribbles and photos into a book.

How to Climb Harder

(Above) Rebecca Williams eyes up the crux on Seamstress (VS), Dinorwic Slate Quarries.

Two identical climbers of equal strength. One of them has good fluid technique, whilst the other relies on their arms. The technician will out climb the thug hands down. Our arms will never be as strong as the rest of our bodies.

This is a practical guide for rock climbers who want to climb harder. It includes exercises that can be carried out at your local climbing wall, crag, boulders or at home to improve all aspects of your climbing. The book is broken down into three parts:

Preparation – before you climb

Technique – moving up

Training – getting in shape

To begin we'll explore the basics of how we learn so that you get the most out of this book. Followed by ropework and safety considerations that every climber needs to be aware of before they start climbing, whether top roping, lead climbing or bouldering.

Next a series of movement techniques introduced through a progressive series of exercises that lead you from simple to more complex movements. Most of the exercises are intended for bottom roping or bouldering so you can drill the moves until they become second nature. The aim of these exercises is to help you climb safer, with more confidence and less effort than before. The technique section also covers both the tactical and mental techniques that you need for lead climbing.

Finally, the section on training starts with various ways to identify your weaknesses and target your training needs. With this in mind there are exercises and drills to improve aspects of strength and fitness which you can fit in around your climbing. The section on training young people will be of interest to any parent or coach – why an adult's training programme shouldn't be applied to a young person. The last chapter covers the basics of nutrition.

LAZY CLIMBING

The underlying ethos is that of 'lazy climbing', through which it is possible to improve your grade through being and staying relaxed, as well as making the movement of climbing as efficient as possible. If you adopt a lazy style to your climbing you will force yourself to be more efficient.

If you have ever watched a truly great climber then the one thing that you will notice above all is the apparent lack of effort that they put into it. Much of the time they will appear extremely relaxed.

An experienced climber uses all of their skill not to be fitter than you or me but to climb more efficiently. They don't have to pull as hard because they are more in balance.

A great climber also draws upon a wealth of experience in the psychological warfare of lead climbing. By regularly stressing themselves, good climbers have developed a coping strategy to deal with those scary situations. This takes time to develop, but none the less you will become conditioned to becoming more comfortable.

You will become a lazy climber with good footwork, balanced body position, efficient weight transfer and a relaxed attitude. Broken down into their most basic elements these skills can be built up through a steady progression into more technical and dynamic movement.

Learning

(Above) Hazel Robson
keeping her cool of Holy,
Holy, Holy (E2), Dali's
Hole, Dinorwic Quarries.

Consider how you learn skills which require hand-eye coordination, movement and balance. How did you gain the skills you have like driving a car or riding a pushbike? When you first learnt these skills, they required concentration as well as coordination. In the filing cabinet of your mind the instructions for driving were put on file, opened and added to every time you drove. As you progressed things became easier and easier. A few years down the line you have so much practice tucked under your belt that your program file for driving no longer needs your conscious attention at all.

The passage from conscious to unconscious participation is illustrated in the learning curve – the further along that curve, the closer you are to reaching your upper limit of performance.

The learning curve. You
can expect to feel like
your ability is decreasing
until you have become
aware of all the hows,
whys and wherefores.

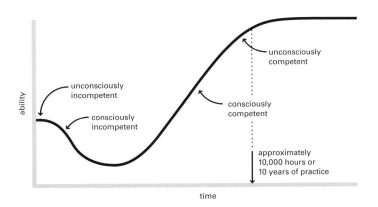

After trying something for the first time we seem to become worse before we get better. At some point we aren't as good at a sport as we initially thought. It is at this point of conscious realisation that we can start to piece together what we are doing wrong and make a decision to improve. The pathways we can take to improvement can be through an informed or an uninformed route.

To take driving, most people have lessons (informed) to be taught how to pass the test, but we also gain experience with friends or relatives (uninformed). The informed progression keeps us heading in the right direction (toward becoming legally safe to drive), but it is often the other experiences and practice that really help us develop.

It takes around one hundred repetitions of a movement to develop muscle memory (unconscious ability). Furthermore, driving or climbing are more than just one or two basic movements. They require you to interact with the real world and to know which skill to pull from your toolbox for any situation.

It is possible to learn how to drive in an empty car park, but the real skill of driving is learning how to interact with other road users, pedestrians, rain, etc. Likewise in climbing it is good to know a series of key movement skills, but it is the ability to pick the right one at the right time that is important. This is the competence that we are aiming to develop, something which might well take ten years or ten thousand hours of practice before you reach your highest level.

To learn a new movement skill we repeat a series of muscular movements and get feedback. After many repetitions we lay down movement memory and our nervous system is conditioned to just how hard, fast and long the muscle has to contract or relax. With experience we will have more movements to call upon and the more frequently we use them the closer to the front of our 'filing cabinet' the movements will be.

Left to develop these skills on your own can lead to bad technique or down dead ends. The exercises in this book will help to combat this and help you to 'listen to' your body as you climb. Efficient climbing comes down to making the right move at the right time, and whilst there are no hard and fast rules, by learning to feel how hard a move is it becomes easier to make improvements to save energy.

Learning isn't just about trying new things; it also requires feedback. What have you learnt? Why you have learnt it? How does that lesson fit into the bigger picture?

In its simplest form the process is Plan – Do – Review. Planning is reading the exercises, looking at the diagrams and thinking about what you are about to do. Doing is the easy part, in doing the exercises our brains are learning things about our bodies, the skills and the movement. Review is when we ask ourselves what we have just learnt, good or bad, how we could improve and perhaps where to go next. It is important to allow yourself some time to review your session and review your planned progress.

The learning spiral. As you work your way out from the centre, your skills accumulate. At times it will be necessary to make backward steps to consolidate your skills.

Bear in mind three things when you practise; try to learn only one thing at a time, keep things simple, discover things for yourself.

*7+/-2 (seven plus or minus two).

Most people can take on board roughly* seven pieces of information before there is too much information to process.

By 'take on board' I mean 'process in short term memory'. Our short term sensory store can process way more than our short term memory, which is the problem.

As part of learning a new skill consider the experience you already have. A gymnast or black belt may not have climbed much rock but they will be quick to learn because they have learnt to feel their body, they have methods for learning new skills and they have developed balance, flexibility and proprioception. As a climber you bring a vast amount of prior learning to the learning cycle, some of which may be bad technique which will need to be undone. No two people will be the same.

Proprioception

Proprioception is the body's ability to take on spatial maps of the environment, in relation to the body. This is perhaps best illustrated by our ability to walk from the door of our bedroom to the bed with the lights off. In climbing it is more about our ability to create a 3D model of the holds and the rock face, as well as how the body can position itself within that map.

Use your warm-up at the start of your session to remind youself what you learnt last time. Open your mental filing cabinet and bring the climbing files to the front.

In order for your practice to be most effective for long term learning the practice needs to be varied and random. Don't train at the same spot on the same things again and again, mix it up in different locations and situations. And by moving location you give yourself some down time from the exercise to process that new information.

Constant repetition during practice will give quick results during your session, but the lessons learnt will fade without breaks to consolidate and think about what you have just done. It is important to take breaks from practice even if it is simply resting whilst a friend climbs.

Practice needs to be bilateral, both left and right or climbing both up and down – variety is the key. Motor skills can be quite specific to each limb (think of kicking a football or snowboarding regular or goofy) and varied movement gives greater diversity to our practice.

Keep on practising. It takes around 100 repetitions of a movement to develop an 'engram' or movement memory. Volume is important.

Efficient practice

Start by repeating an exercise in isolation on one problem.

Move onto repeating that exercise in varied and random situations.

Break/pause to think.

Be bilateral (up/down and left/right).

Volume – around 100 repetitions to develop movement memory

Above all your time spent practising needs to be sound as bad practice will lead to bad technique. If you find yourself getting tired or you fail repeatedly then stop and rest or move on to something else.

Practice does not make perfect, only perfect practice makes perfect – Dr John Fazey

Safety First

(Above) James McHaffie
fully aware of the risks of
climbing on Craig Doris,
where it is impossible
to avoid loose and falling
rock! It takes expert
judgement as to which
holds will take body
weight and which won't.

This may seem like teaching your grandmother to suck eggs, but taking time to increase your awareness of risk is often overlooked. It's common sense. When you look at a hazard (like being high off the ground) and the risk (of falling) you will consider ways to reduce the risk.

Many of the dangers at the crag can affect the climber, the belayer and even bystanders. So it is important to keep an eye on the situation around you as it develops and adapt your plans to suit. The key to climbing safely at the beginning of your climbing career is to choose the right crag, grade and route.

(Left) Subliminal at Swanage;
a single pitch venue with
easy routes but all the routes
require an abseil approach.
Additional rope skills are
needed to escape, as
casualties cannot be lowered
off and carried away.
(Right) A festive ascent of
Christmas Crack, Stanage
Edge; solid rock, easy access
to the top and bottom. This
crag is often extremely
busy. Photo | John Foster.

Choosing the right climb may seem difficult. Guidebooks are a starting point but local knowledge can be invaluable, so talk to people you meet at the crag or wall, the sales assistant in an outdoor shop and instructors or outdoor centres; most will happily give advice on venues. Eventually you need to assess a crag or a route's suitability for yourself. Often, just by being aware of a hazard will greatly reduce the risk of an accident.

It is the risks you don't know you're taking that are likely to kill you.

We'll consider a simple break-down of top roping, lead climbing and bouldering; the hazards, the likelihood of an accident, and any measures we can take to reduce the risk and the residual risk after we've taken action. Many of these things are common sense. You may find the technical side of climbing daunting but by becoming more aware of risk, ropework and sound judgement you'll become a safer climber. With regular practice these skills will become second nature. Spend time learning ropework and safety skills from a professional instructor or centre. This is one area of your climbing for which there is no substitute for informed instruction.

RISK: TOP ROPING

Top roping (or bottom roping) is how most people start out climbing and, in the context of this book, one of the most appropriate ways to repeat the exercises in safety. If done properly, it should be a very low risk activity. There are however several fundamental principles that you can learn whilst top roping, that are carried through to lead climbing.

The hazards of top roping, what you can do about them and their overall contribution to the risk of top rope climbing.

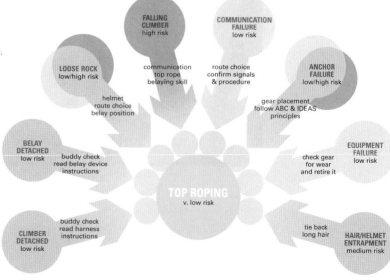

When you're top roping, avoid the three-star classic routes, move route regularly (don't use the same route for more than a couple of hours) and make sure you're all wearing rock shoes (you'll climb better and they don't polish the rock like trainers). Groups who monopolise routes, particularly with top ropes, have earned a bad name at busy crags like Stanage.

The safe rigging of a belay for a top or bottom rope requires you to consider some fundamental principles as well as ways to avoid problems. These principles apply right through to the more advanced belays you will come across on multi-pitch climbs.

The ABC of belays

The first step when rigging top ropes is your ABC; **Anchors**, **Belay** and **Climber**. To keep the forces in-line with gravity all three should be in-line to prevent either the belay, belayer or the climber being pulled sideways across the cliff. If the belay is pulled across the cliff edge it may result in damage to the rope and/or unequal loads on the anchors, and if it occurs repeatedly or on a sharp edge it may well cut through the ropes!

A well set up bottom rope with anchors, belay and climber all in a line.

Good setups with (A) anchors, (B) belayer and (C) climber linked with rope and all in line with the direction of pull (gravity). The first two might represent a top rope setup and the third represents a bottom rope setup.

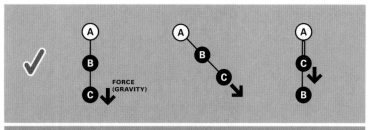

Bad setups. Because the anchor is a fixed point, when the load (gravity) comes on the climber, the belayer may be dragged sideways or down.

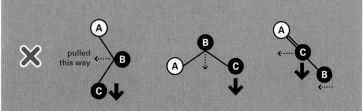

17

The IDEAS principles

The second acronym, which will help to guide you whilst building a safe belay, is IDEAS:

Ticking all the boxes and fulfilling the fundamental principles. This bottom rope setup has the **Anchors**, **Belay** and **Climber** all in line and pulling the anchors in the right direction. The anchors are linked to make them **Independent**, **Directional** and **Equalised**; on top of all this the **Angle** between the anchors is acute and the anchors are **Solid**.

Independent – each of the anchors should connect separately to the belay so if one anchor fails the others won't be shock loaded. This is an important principle to follow throughout the system when linking of anchors with either slings or rope.

(A) Although the sling is self equalising, failure of one anchor will shock load the other. (B) Tied with an overhand knot, this sling is equalised and independent; should an anchor fail there will be no shock load on the other.

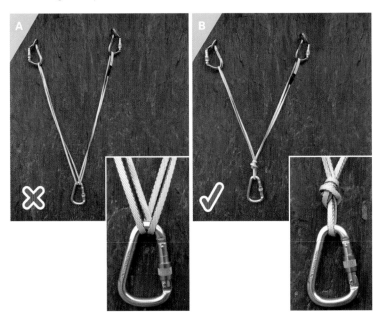

(C) The rope is self equalising but should one anchor fail the karabiner will slip off the rope! (D) A figure of 8 on the bight makes this rope equalised and the anchors independent.

Directional – the anchors, belay and rope should be placed ready to take a load in the direction that any force on the belay will occur. In a top rope this will typically be towards the cliff edge and directly down. If the anchors are pulled in the wrong direction, they may not withstand the load.

(1) A good anchor made poor by an inappropriate direction of pull. (2) A good anchor, with a questionable directional of pull. (3) A good anchor, with the directional of pull appropriate to the placement.

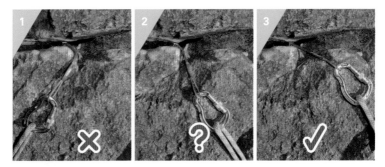

Equalised – any link between your anchors should be under equal tension when loaded in the direction that will result from a fall. Done well, this will share the load equally between the anchors and reduce the chance of anchor failure, and also help to prevent a shock load should one of your anchors fail.

(E) Poorly equalised sling. Only one anchor is bearing weight and if it fails the other will be shock loaded (inset) this arrangement might be equalised with a different angle of pull). (F) Well equalised slings.

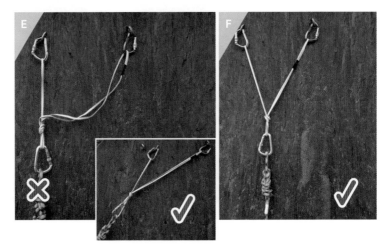

Angles – the angle between the two outside anchors should be kept to a minimum. The smaller the angle the better the force is shared. An acute (narrow) angle is good, a right-angle is alright and an obtuse (wide) angle is bad. Under 60° the load is shared roughly 50% onto each anchor, by 90° the load is shared at 70% onto each anchor, whilst over 120° the load exerted on each anchor is 100% or more of the load (so the benefit of having two anchors share the load is lost). So in practice when anchors are linked with rope or slings the greatest angle between anchors should not exceed 90°.

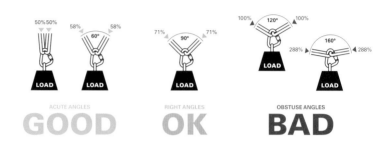

ACUTE ANGLES
GOOD

RIGHT ANGLES
OK

OBSTUSE ANGLES
BAD

Solid – reliable anchors are the key to any belay. Check the rock surrounding your placements to ensure that the rock is not hollow or loose. Tap the rock with a karabiner and if it sounds hollow look elsewhere. The placements you choose should be as good as possible (see the section on gear placement page 27).

A good nut placement? Close inspection reveals a hairline crack (just above the karabiner) that runs across the bottom of the flake, making the placement questionable, as the flake may be detached and fail when shock loaded.

Equalising slings and ropes

Practise your rigging at home.

To get your ABC and IDEAS right, you'll need to be able to equalise the loads on your slings or rope. There are many ways to achieve this, each has pros and cons, and some will be more efficient than others in certain situations.

Equalising a sling exercise –

Try rigging the three systems on this page and see if they tick all the IDEAS principles; this can be done either at the bottom of a crag or at home on the stairs or off the legs of a dining table. Then unclip each anchor in turn to see if the system remains equalised and in-line (no shock loading). Practise in a variety of places with different anchors.

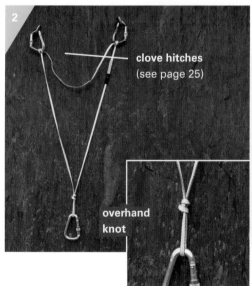

clove hitches
(see page 25)

overhand
knot

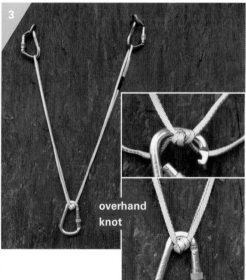

overhand
knot

Both of these equalised slings do the job of bringing two belay points to one. One uses more of the length of the sling than the other.

Clip the karabiner into the sling both sides of the knot. In essence the knot has created a sling either side of the knot.

Use anchor points further apart; what happens to the angles? Are they more or less than 90°. Does one method make a smaller angle than the other? Does one become harder to tie than the other?

The bigger the distance from anchor to anchor, the bigger the angle. Find a way to keep the angle below 90°.

 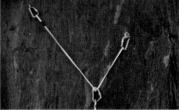

How we equalise anchors depends on the direction of expected load. This time find some new anchors to equalise the slings for a straight down pull, then a leftward and rightward pull.

Whilst equalising a sling is very useful, using the rope to join anchors together to a single point is the backbone of building a belay.

Equalising a rope exercise – Look at the diagram below and recreate this belay (A) off two anchors. Tie off one end of the rope to the first anchor, then flick out a loop of rope so it sits just over the edge, and tie the loop off back to a clove hitch. Similar to the exercise with slings the two points are made independent by adding a figure of eight knot (rather than an overhand knot). Then recreate the belay (B) with three anchors (with so many ropes a simple overhand can be used to bring everything together).

Edge protection

On top of the fundamentals of ABC and IDEAS there are additional considerations that can make the system easier to use and safer. We will want to avoid the rope running over the rock, rubbing away at the fibres of the rope and possible jamming in nooks or crannies. As they are weighted and unweighted a sawing action can affect short sections of rope where they repeatedly rub the rock. This can be minimised by using a static rigging rope for the anchors rather than dynamic climbing rope.

A simple two point anchor bottom roping system tied with a red rigging rope.

The well rigged belay point is over the edge of the cliff. No extra rope drag and reducing the chance of the rope jamming in a nook or cranny.

(Inset) Poor rigging like this will produce excessive rope drag (friction), damaging your ropes and even the rock.

Where rope rubbing on an edge is unavoidable use an edge protector, anything from a jumper, jacket or rucksack will do (nb. these will be damaged, but left with a choice of a cut rope or a worn out pullover what would you choose?) Off-cuts of carpet or door mats make good edge protectors and there are even some specially designed rope collars.

(A) There is a point of wear wherever a rope moves over an edge. As the rigging rope is repeatedly weighted and unweighted, causing a sawing action, rope rubbing against the edge may be cut or damaged.

(B) Rope cut on a sharp edge.

(C) The top edge of a sandstone crag, Damaged by poorly rigged bottom ropes. Bottom roping and lowering off is now banned at some venues to prevent further damage to the climbs, as such the climber often has to top out, untie, and walk down.

(D) Prevent excessive wear on your ropes with a rope collar (hose pipe cut length ways works well).

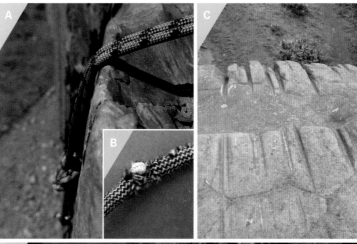

Using the rope you're climbing on to build the belay

This system is one of the most practical in terms of 'real' climbing – using the rope tied to us to rig a belay as we would if we had just led a pitch. It also has the advantage early on that you don't need both a rigging rope and a rope for climbing on.

> **Top roping system exercise** – Try out each of the five ways to clip into one anchor on the opposite page. You will need to be familiar with how to tie a clove hitch.

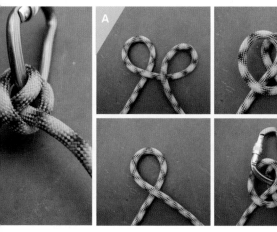

(A) Tie a clove hitch to a karabiner, with practice you can get very slick at this. Experiment with this versatile hitch.

(B) When adjusting the clove hitch that is attached to you, pull the loop and the slack away from you to ensure it stays snug.

The clove hitch – Tie the clove hitch to a single anchor and adjust it so you are snug, now try to pay some rope out and move further from the anchor (make sure the rope is snug). Then move back in and take in the slack.

Now clip a loop of rope through anchor and clove hitch it to a screw-gate on your belay loop. Try adjusting distance from the anchor and back towards it. With this method you can easily adjust the tension on the rope when out of reach of the anchors.

Here are five different ways to tie into a one point anchor. Tie each one and experiment with adjusting your distance from the anchor. These are the building blocks for the next exercise.

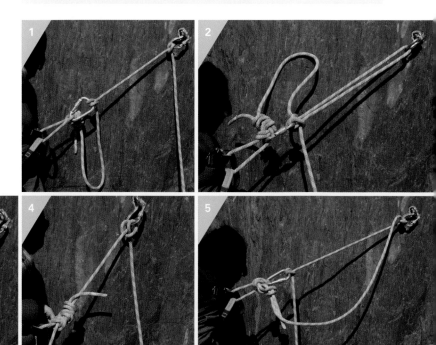

This exercise will help you to choose how to go about tying into your anchors. Some of the combinations simply don't work. Discover which of them are useful by trying each of them out and your belay skills will be much more robust.

Skilful belays exercise – Now tie into two anchors. If possible totally change the configuration of the anchors between each attempt. Work through the following permutations of the five tying in methods shown, some will work well together others won't.

1+2, 1+3, 1+4, 1+5, 2+3, 2+4, 2+5, 3+4, 3+5, 4+5

Does it make a difference tying into these left to right compared to right to left? How does the distance from the anchors effect tying into each of these systems? Which system uses the most rope? What works? In order to answer these question you will have to experiment, and by the end of it your brain will be fried into one very big knot so allow some time to process all the information before moving on with this exercise, I might even suggest sleeping on it!

It's important to get the tension equal to each of the two anchors. Pick a spot at which you wish to end up after you have tied into the anchors. Use a variety of anchors including close, distant, high and low. Try out the different methods to make a well tensioned belay on your chosen spot. Sit down to see how it effects the direction of pull on the anchors.

Ask yourself; is it safe, under equal tension and efficient? Can you see a way to improve it? Does it fit IDEAS and ABC?

Tying into at least one anchor when approaching the edge (with a clove hitch).

WARNING – When rigging a climb you are at times un-roped at the top of a substantial drop. It may be necessary to make yourself safe. When setting up a bottom rope this may include clove hitching into one anchor as you approach the edge. This is not a bombproof system so don't deliberately weight it, but it may prevent a slip becoming a fall. If it is a top rope setup, consider having one anchor a reasonable distance back and tie into this, again don't weight the system until all points are equalised and under tension.

If you need to approach the edge un-roped bear in mind that a gust of wind or a slip might lead to tragic consequences. So always imagine that at any point an invisible person might come and nudge you. By laying or sitting down you can prevent a fall, alternatively keep a low stance and have good hand hold at all times.

In reach/out of reach – Often you'll be either in reach or out of reach of the anchors you want to tie into; either way you need to work systematically, decide first where you need to stand to belay, then clip the first rope in and adjust the clove hitch so you are snug, only then go on and clip the rope into the second anchor and adjust the clove hitch.

Tying into (A) two anchors within reach, (B) a single out of reach anchor and (C) two anchors which are out of reach.

Gear placements

Placing good runners and anchors is the foundation of safe ropework. Your other efforts are futile if the anchors are all going to fail. A placement will only be as good as the rock it's in, loose rock and superficial flakes will be poor placements. Follow the three 'S's when placing gear:

Solid – is the rock integral to the placement solid?

Shape – is the shape of the placement suitable for the gear choice?

Size – is the gear the right size for the placement?

Several sizes of nut in good tapering vertical cracks.

Nuts, wires and rocks

A rack of wires,
sizes 1 to 11.

The original running belay placement for cracks were simply small pebbles or stones placed by climber as chockstones and threaded with a sling; over time climbers started to drill out machine nuts and use them instead. Now various companies make a variety of different shaped and sized wedges on wire rope.

When correctly placed at a natural constriction in the crack the nut will be unable to pull through. When placing a nut you need to consider several things.

Quality of the rock – avoid using loose or hollow sounding rock, along with superficial flakes. Check the rock by tapping it with a karabiner, a hollow sound will indicate poorer quality. If it is a flake try moving it by giving it a good shake, or hitting the flake with the palm of one hand whilst feeling for vibrations with the other. However you check the rock remember that you are at the top of a cliff and possibly unroped, and there may be people below you, so take care not to send anything over the edge of the cliff, especially yourself.

Three ways to check
the integrity of the
placement; using the
palm of the hand to
knock the flake and
feel for vibrations or
movement, giving
it a good shake and
seeing if it moves and
tapping and listening
for a hollow sound.

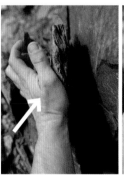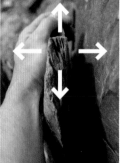

Natural constriction – to select a good nut placement, you first need to identify cracks in line with the route you are climbing. You then need to find a natural constriction in that crack where a nut can be wedged in, and won't pull through. There may be signs of smoothing/wear and tear on popular climbs, often but not always an indication of a good placement.

The same nut and crack
with, (left) a large surface
area of the nut in contact
with the rock and (right)
a poorer placement with
less surface area of the nut
in contact with the rock.

Contact area – when the nut is securely wedged in the crack the greater the surface area of the nut in contact with the rock the better the placement. Try simply turning the wire round or a different sized wire.

Overlap – when the nut is securely in place there needs to be a reasonable overlap between the width of the crack and the width of the nut. The reason for this is that if there is an extreme load on the placement it may simply pull the nut through the placement.

The same placement with (left) a good overlap between the size of crack and nut and (right) a bad overlap, the nut may well pull through under extreme load.

Seating – does the gear stay put when left alone? First you must seat the nut securely. Use the other wires on your rack of wires as a grip and create a shock load by jerking in the direction of pull on the wire. The nut will probably move slightly in the placement and hopefully drop into a snug fit. Then if you lightly wiggle the wire you will see if it unseats itself from the placement; a well-seated nut will stay secure. Try not to over-do this, as you may end up with your gear stuck in the crack, impossible to remove.

Get into the habit of jerking the wires into place to seat your wires so that, if the wire pulls through when you jerk it, only your arm moves. If you pull with your body weight to seat a wire and the placement fails, you will fall away from the rock with it!

Jerking the wire to seat it in place. You can exert more force on the nut by shock loading it in this way than if you sat your weight slowly on the nut.

Hexes and Tri-cams

The judgement we need to select a Hex or Tri-cam placement is very similar to selecting a nut placement. How they are placed is slightly different. Both Hexes and Tri-cams can be placed as passive nuts. However they are designed to cam into placement and become more secure the greater the load placed on them. It is also important to seat them in the placement by applying a shock load by jerking down on the tape.

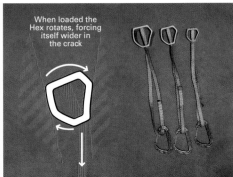

When loaded the Hex rotates, forcing itself wider in the crack

(Above) Two Hex placements

When either a Hex or a Tri-cam is loaded the resultant force makes the device twist in the crack, and in doing so making them wider, and less likely to fail. Tri-cams work well in horizontal breaks. A Tri-cam can also be arranged in vertical cracks and in the shot-holes often found in quarried rock.

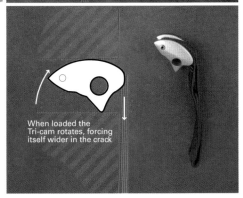

When loaded the Tri-cam rotates, forcing itself wider in the crack

Spikes and threads

The hierarchy of runners: When placing a runner look for placements roughly in this order of strongest to weakest:
1 Spikes, threads and trees
2 Nuts and Hexes
3 Camming devices

When using spikes and threads as forms of protection you need to consider the three 'S's again. As a general rule of thumb a free standing boulder needs to be at least twice the size of an adult curled up in a ball, as well as in a position where it can't be pulled over the edge. For the scientist one cubic metre of rock is about 2 tonnes.

The shape of the spike needs to be angled back away from the direction of force so that the sling or rope that is a round the spike doesn't ride up over the top and off the spike. To check this make a sawing motion with sling or rope in the direction of the likely load. If it rides up the placement will be compromised.

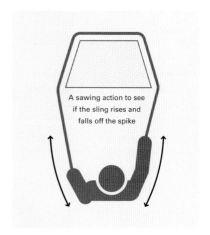

A sawing action to see
if the sling rises and
falls off the spike

A variety of good and bad shaped spikes. Testing the spike by making a sawing motion with the sling.

Like any placement, a spike will only be any good if it is solid. To check for this at first try rocking the boulder, but be aware that if it on the edge of a cliff, it might topple off onto people! If it doesn't move, try giving it a kick with your foot and feel for vibrations in your hand.

In the case of spikes that are part of the mountain, the size of the flake is often unimportant. It will just be the shape and solidity that are vital.

Metal spikes, pegs and bolts

A spike tied off lower down to reduce the leverage on the spike. Tie a clove hitch or take a wrap of the sling around the spike, to prevented the sling from slipping upwards.

Back up in situ metal protection where possible with other protection. Metal spikes and pegs will be most corroded below the surface and whilst you can test to see if it's wobbly there is little more you can do to check how sound it may be. Rust may appear superficial but hidden below it may have taken hold. Tying off the spike or peg as low as possible will minimise the leverage on it.

Bolts are a little different as there may be notes on their history in a guidebook. Knowing when the bolt was placed and what type it is will help your judgement. Stainless steel is less likely to corrode than plain steel. Resin bolts have a longer life span than simple expansion bolts. Some of the bolts on crags are little more than 8mm thick and 30mm long and may have been in place for over twenty years. If the bolts are subject to the salty conditions of a maritime environment, treat them with further caution.

Newer bolts (top) rely on stainless steel throughout. Compare it to the old stainless steel hanger and small ordinary steel bolt (bottom), which caused greater levels of corrosion. Which would you prefer to hang off?

Hanger (A) is made of aluminium and has become badly corroded.
Hanger (B) is made of steel, the ring is stainless and placed with a stainless steel bolt by accident it has corroded quickly; this one was removed from a route after only two months of exposure.

Using different metals or alloys for the bolt, nut and hanger can cause an electrolytic reaction which will rapidly corrode one part or other. If the bolt has signs of rust and the hanger doesn't its an indication of mixed metals reacting with each other. Some aluminium hangers react with the bolt, resulting in oxidisation.

Trees

Trees, like spikes, are great placements but not many climbers are experienced tree surgeons so it is difficult to be sure of them. First look up; the tree should look alive, with either leaves or in the mist of winter some fresh buds or healthy looking branches. Then look down to see if the roots look healthy and strong. As a rule of thumb the thinnest diameter of trunk that is suitable for using as a anchor is roughly the thickness of your thigh. If it as thick as your waist then it could be used as a single point anchor. As with metal spikes, tying around a tree low down will reduce the leverage on it.

A healthy tree with new shoots of leaves. In winter look for healthy buds or fresh shoots of leaves.

Cams

Camming devices are the most complicated piece of gear to place well, but they can offer solid protection in parallel sided cracks where there would otherwise be none. The most important consideration is that when loaded the device will produce a large force (about 3 to 4 times the load placed on them) that will try and force the placement apart, they may well lever off a flake, so the integrity of the rock is paramount.

There are other important considerations when placing cams: The direction of pull should be along the shaft of the camming device; all the cams should also be in contact with the rock; and the cams should be somewhere well within the maximum and minimum width of the camming device (ie. between 25% and 75% of the full range of movement).

(A) Under cammed, the device is 'tipped out', hanging by the tips of the cams, which makes the placement weaker. Choose a larger cam for this crack.

(B) A well placed cam, neither over or under cammed. Ideally placed the cams should rest somewhere between 25% and 75% of their range,

(C) Over cammed, the device has been forced into a placement that is too small. The placement is weaker and the cam may become jammed.

Gear placing exercise – Walk round the bottom of a crag, practising each of the types of gear placement and discuss with friends how you rate them from 0 to 5:

0 – You would hang your worse enemy's jacket on it

1 – You would hang your jacket on it

2 – You would hang your enemy on it

3 – You would hang off it

4 – You would hang your enemy's car off it

5 – You would hang your car off it

Safe belaying

Safe and effective belaying is as important as the anchors and system at the top of the crag. Every year numerous people are injured both inside and out when they are dropped by their belayer. Belaying correctly requires concentration and communication by both belayer and climber. Avoid distractions whilst climbing; eating your sandwiches, drinking a flask of coffee or holding a conversation can take your mind off the job at hand. Belaying properly requires both hands and all your attention.

Never take a hand off the dead rope! On early practices it is best to have someone backing up the dead rope to ensure there are no nasty accidents.

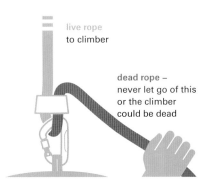

live rope
to climber

dead rope –
never let go of this
or the climber
could be dead

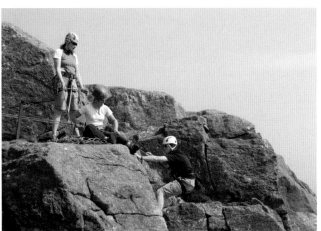

Belaying a bottom rope – You will need some coaching from an experienced climber, for the first few times have someone tail the dead rope until you are ready to do it alone. Many climbers introducing friends to climbing have been dropped at both indoor walls and crags, whilst the novice remains safe but unsupervised belaying from the ground. The most important thing is to never let go of the 'dead rope' whilst taking in slack as the climber ascends.

Belaying a bottom rope sequence.

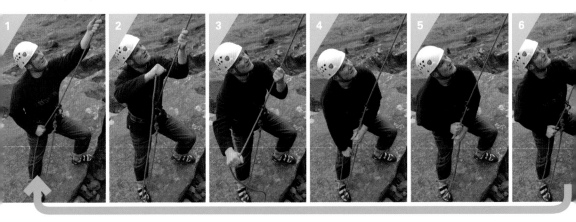

Very soon you will be able to shorten this in your head to: 'Take in', 'Lock off', 'Hand swap'. Breaking down the bottom rope sequence into three chunks.

1. Prepare to take in the rope.

2. Take in the rope, pulling the rope through the device with both hands.

3. Lock the rope off.

4. Move both hands to the dead rope.

5. Swap the bottom hand to starting position below the belay plate.

6. Go to step 1.

The climber may climb faster than a belayer can take rope in, resulting in a lot of slack; if the climber falls there will be a considerable drop before the rope and gear is shock loaded. If you are climbing, slow down when you notice too much slack; if you're belaying, ask the climber to pause whilst you catch up.

When the climber reaches the top you need a simple procedure; talking to each other, making the rope tight before lowering the climber down. Repeating the same procedure time and again reinforces the trust between climber and belayer and reduces the likelihood of an accidental drop as the climber weighs the rope.

Lower-off procedure

1. The climber gets to the top and calls to belayer, "TAKE IN". The climber should look down to see if the belayer is taking in and if possible make eye contact to confirm the belayer has heard.

2. The belayer takes in rope and looks to see if it is tight on the climber. As the belayer feels the rope go tight they shout, "IS THAT YOU?"

3. The climber feels the rope go tight and looks to ensure the belayer has locked off, then keeping a hand on the rope going down to the belayer as a back up, lowers their weight onto the rope slowly, when you have committed your weight to the rope and are happy that you are being held, shout "THAT'S ME".

4. The belayer pauses, shouts "OK" and then starts to lower the climber in a slow and controlled fashion.

Belaying at the top of the cliff – This may seem a simple thing to do but it's not completely straightforward. At times you will need to be able to belay both left and right handed so you will need to practise both sides. If you belay with the wrong hand you simply can't get the required angle of lock on the belay plate which means you get considerably less friction.

The first thing is your stance; whether sitting or standing you need to be side-on with whichever hand is closest to the anchors as the hand you will lock off with. Make sure that your belay plate is aligned, so the dead rope (the one you lock off) is coming out of the appropriate side of the plate and the live rope (the one going to the climber) comes out the downwards or outward side of the belay.

Having established the correct stance and aligned the belay plate correctly the pattern of belaying is similar to that when belaying from the bottom. The simple version is to (1) take the rope in. (2) lock the rope off. (3) hand swap. (4) back to the beginning.

Remember that the first time you do this, just like the belaying a top rope, you need someone to tail the dead rope as a backup. Preferably someone experienced and sitting down back from the edge.

(A) Sitting side-on the climbers left hand is closest to the belay so that hand will lock off and control the dead rope. The belay plate aligned correctly, with the dead rope going up towards the anchors.

(B) An incorrectly aligned belay plate means you cannot lock off properly.

The simple belaying pattern is the same: 1, Take the rope in. 2, Lock the rope off. 3, Swap hands. 4, Back to the beginning. Remember never let go of the dead rope.

Buddy system

The human factor is a major contributor to many accidents and near misses in so many situations. I have seen experienced climbers forget to do their harness up, not tie in correctly, attach a belay plate to their gear loop and other silly mistakes. A buddy systems has stopped any of these becoming an accident. Make safety a team effort when building belays, belaying, tying in or putting on your harness. We all make mistakes and a simple mistake can have catastrophic consequences. By checking and double checking each other and the whole system you will help prevent anyone making any stupid mistakes. This is a basic principle which helps build trust between climbing partners, knowing someone is watching your back and that you must watch theirs.

Belay devices

Belay devices have evolved from early stitch plates that were just a piece of metal with a hole in. The now more common tubular designs have a greater surface area to dissipate the heat that builds up during a long lower or abseil. Some more recent advancements are the adding of grooves or offsetting where the karabiner rests. Both designs help add friction to the system, making the device grip the rope harder, making locking off of the rope easier. The variety of belay devices is seemingly endless. Used correctly any brand or model should be adequate, however some are more slick than others and a few are (semi) auto-locking.

Evolution of belay plate – (A) sprung stitch plate. (B) DMM Buggette for use with thin 8mm ropes. (C) a Metolius BRD with an offset karabiner alignment. (D) a DMM V-Twin with grooves. (E) Petzl Reverso which can be used in a variety of ways. (F) an auto-locking belay device the Gri-Gri, which still requires careful and proper belaying, as well as even more care when lowering climbers.

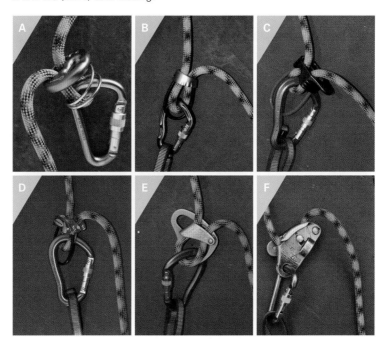

Although dubbed 'auto-locking', devices like the Petzl Gri-Gri don't work every time. Generally they will lock the rope in the event of a fall, but you still need to manage the dead rope correctly as they cannot be fully relied on. Auto-locking devices also have the disadvantage of being more complicated to lower a climber, so you should read the instructions carefully and practise with a climber close to the ground.

Harnesses

Which harness you use comes down to fit and comfort. The only advice worth considering is what you intend to use the harness for; traditional, sport, alpine and winter climbing have different requirements. It is far cheaper to start with to get a good multipurpose harness with adjustable leg loops.

Generally the choices are type of gear loop, adjustable leg loops and what type of buckle the harness has. Some harness are specifically designed with women in mind and one manufacturer has even created a harness, where every part of the harness is rated to at least 10kN, after a series of accidents where people have inadvertently clipped into their gear loops, normally only rated at a few kilos. The risk of this can be lessened by keeping your belay device clipped to a rear gear loop, so you have to unclip it and move it to the appropriate place for belaying (not the front gear loop!)

A great all rounder, with plenty of gear loops for leading even the most demanding of routes, a floating tie-in point and adjustable leg loops.

Climbing big routes on mountain crags and sea cliffs can require large racks; your harness might need to be able to accommodate this. Two gear loops on either side is the minimum for traditional climbing.

Helmets

Whilst not essential, wearing a helmet is a good idea. A crag may not appear to have much loose rock but there may be some hidden up on ledges waiting for a passing climber or a rope to knock it over the edge. A climber above you could simply drop a piece of climbing gear. Should you fall, a helmet will help to protect your head if you hit the wall or deck out.

Absent Friends (E5 6a) Craig Doris – even experts wear helmets. Climber, Sam Underfoot.

Old arguments of heavy cumbersome helmets that were impractical simply don't wash anymore and whilst the lighter the helmet, the less protection there is, they all reach UIAA guidelines, so offer better protection than no helmet at all.

...any helmet is better than no helmet.

The helmet you feel comfortable in is the best helmet as you are more likely wear it all the time. Discomfort may tempt you to remove your helmet.

'I once was one of the first climbers on the scene of a nasty accident where a climber had tumbled 50 metres down a descent gully. He had quite neatly clipped his helmet to his harness at the top of the climb. When he was airlifted to hospital they discovered he had fractured his skull in the tumble and took months to recover. What would have happened if he had been wearing his helmet?'

Rock shoes

Dirty shoes will not grip well. Get into the habit of cleaning the soles and drying them thoroughly before climbing. A bit of spit and the palm of your hand is often enough to make them squeaky clean. If they get dirty or wet on the route then wipe them on the inside leg of your trousers.

For young climbers having over-tight shoes has lead to permanent foot deformity in later life. Children need to be at least 15 before they start cramming their feet into under sized shoes (see the chapter Training: The Young Climber).

There is a profusion of shoes to choose from. At first you are better off going for comfort, rather than performance, although a reasonably tight pair will pay dividends with your footwork. Generally one model of shoes will fit you better than the others, so don't go on recommendations, try on lots of different makes and models until you find the right shoe for you.

Some shoes are designed specifically for different types of climbing. A stiff midsole makes for good performance if you are going to climb on edges like slate. A soft midsole makes for a shoe that is suited for smearing on rock like gritstone. Many modern rock shoes have a drop toe configuration; these are great for steep or pocketed like limestone or bouldering. To start off with you are better getting an all round shoe rather than a specialist shoe.

Chalk bags

There are many chalk bags which all do a similar job, the main thing is to make sure it is big enough to get your hand into, not just the finger tips. The chalk you use is a matter of personal choice, although indoors a chalk ball prevents the air becoming filled with chalk dust.

(A) Well attached chalk bag, high and able to slide to the side. (B) Poorly attached chalk bag which will hang low and cannot be slid towards the hand you need to chalk.

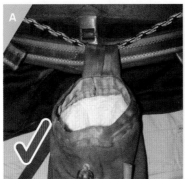 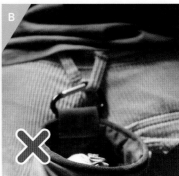

People attach the chalk bag to them a in a variety of ways by a karabiner, specialist belt or cord. The belt or cord attachments are best at giving a high position of the chalk bag and also allowing you to move the chalk bag to the front or side if in a tight corner, groove or chimney.

EQUIPMENT CARE

There are various standards that each and every piece of protective equipment must pass for it to be fit for purpose and saleable, often involving randomized destruction testing during manufacture. After some use and abuse you'll need to decide when to retire and replace your equipment.

General rule of thumb on equipment life -- Metal equipment has a life-span of up to ten years. For webbing allow five years storage (on shop shelf) and then five years use. Ropes should be retired before five years from the date of manufacture. It is important to realise that heavy use will reduce these life spans

There is anecdotal evidence that metalwork in particular can withstand the test of time. DMM tested a featherlight karabiner from the 1960s which still broke at 20kN, similarly they have run 'Break what you Brung' workshops at various events and have found twenty year old karabiners regularly breaking at their cited strength. Aluminium hardens with age, which also means that a new wire is slightly plastic and may mould itself to a crack when you fall on it, but an older wire may not. Whilst this shouldn't compromise the placement it is an interesting consequence of metal ageing.

Checking the wire rope on some nuts for damage. (Top right) a brass nut showing corrosion. (Bottom) three rejected nuts showing damaged wire strands.

Check your wires regularly, by examining the swaged wire rope for damage. If any of the strands are broken then it is time to replace it (the strength will be affected and the sharp wire may abrade your webbing or rope). Slide the metal wedge down the wire to see what is going on underneath it too.

It is a myth that if you drop a karabiner on the floor from the slightest height it may magically hit a sweet spot, causing micro-fractures and compromising the integrity of the karabiner. Aluminium karabiners are forged at over 400 degrees centigrade so the metal forms strong molecular bonds that are elastic. However if you drop a piece of gear down an entire pitch and it lands on solid rock then you would be advised to retire it.

All metalwork is liable to corrosion especially if you climb at or near the coast. Salt in the air will stick to the metal and stay there slowly corroding the metal whilst it languishes in your rucksack until the salt is washed away. Rinse all hardware in fresh water and allow to air dry after climbing at sea cliffs, to limit corrosion. Gear is often anodised, which creates a barrier to corrosion; however, any scratch to the anodised surface exposes the metal underneath to the corrosive environment, so even anodised equipment needs a rinse.

Cams (with all their moving parts) need to be regularly cleaned and lubricated with a light oil like Metolius cam oil or Duck oil. They can also be cleaned with Metolius cam cleaner. This will prevent them from seizing up. Oil the axle which the cams rotate around and make sure all the cams move independently of the axle and each other. Sometimes a long fall onto a cam or dirt will stop the cams moving independently, making the cam less stable when placed. Also the trigger wires can break but these can often be replaced by the manufacturer for a small charge. If the unit is over ten years old they will not replace the trigger/wires or re-sling the cam.

Both cams and Hexes have webbing slings, which will have a life span shorter than the metal parts. These can be replace by the manufacturer at a price. Webbing is more susceptible to damage from UV light and also abrades quickly. Abrasion causes more damage than you might imagine. Destruction tests show that a new Dyneema sling, which has been cut through ⅓ of the width of the sling, and abraded across its whole width elsewhere, will snap first where it is abraded before it tears at the cut. This is why the five year rule of thumb is best understood as a maximum life span, as heavy use will result in abrasion all over the sling.

Harnesses may also suffer abrasion, general wear and tear as well as specific wear points (where the buckles are tightened and loosened every time we put a harness on and take it off and also where the rope is threaded through the strong point of the harness).

A worn harness was the cause of the death of Todd Skinner, a famous and experienced climber, who had ordered a new harness that hadn't arrived prior to his climbing trip.

Your rope too needs to be inspected and maintained (a rope's life span of five years is also best understood as a maximum). Heavy use or being weighted over an edge may damage the sheath of the rope or the core. If the damage is severe then retire the rope. You should check your rope every time you use it (you probably do this without realising). As you flake the rope out, feel it run through your hands, checking for fluffy sections or irregularities in the rope, then examine these section more thoroughly. If it feels like the core is damaged then it is better to replace the rope than risk your life.

This rope looked fine when it was taken out on a multi-pitch climb in the mountains. During the day the climbers decided to lower off the route. The rope ran over a sharp edge and the sheath of the rope was badly damage. The rope was retired but note that there is little damage to the core that makes up around 90% of the strength of the rope.

Don't treat your rope badly – don't step on it, dry it after use if it gets wet, wash it from time to time in fresh water and don't add your own half way marks with marker pens (which may damage the sheath).

Whilst UV will damage sheath of the rope just like webbing and slings, it is less of an issue with rope as the sheath contributes about 10% of the overall strength, the remaining 90% is provided by the core. Recent tests of in situ abseil tat exposed to an alpine environment has shown that compared to slings the reduction in strength is not as dramatic or dangerous as slings exposed to UV. Store your rope away from direct sunlight.

RISK: LEAD CLIMBING

You would probably put placing gear and building belays high on your list of skills needed for safe lead climbing (skills you will have begun to develop from top roping). There are some additional skills you need to consider.

Belaying a lead climber.

Belaying a second (belayer at top of pitch).

Judging a route against your ability.

Assessing the dangers of a route.

Understanding and following guidebook descriptions.

Moving efficiently over the rock.

Abseiling and escaping from the climb.

Quite a few more hazards to think about than there were for top rope climbing (see page 16).

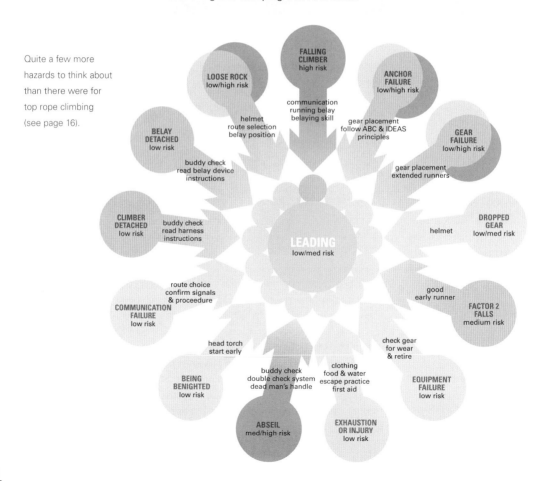

Climbing safety systems are most often aimed at stopping the consequences of a slip or a fall. In lead climbing, especially when starting out, consider what you can do to prevent a fall in the first place. Choose the right route that suits your style and ability and which you already know. More often than not the psychological pressures put on you during lead climbing have a negative effect on your climbing ability. Be aware of these pressures and the consequences of a fall. Taking a lead fall on an easy route often means that there are ledges and slabs to hit on the way down. The chances of injury are higher falling off an easier route than they are on a steeper route with equal protection (but the chance of falling off in the first place is lower). The best way to prevent injuries from falls is not to fall off.

"the leader never falls"

old maxim from the days of tying in by wrapping a hemp rope
around your waist in a swami belt.

You can help yourself to reduce the fall by down climbing and also warning the belayer that you are about to fall. Often it is best to accept the fall and jump off rather than fall and slide down the rock.

No matter how well chosen your route, there will come a point when you will overstretch yourself and be unable to go up or down. At this point you will want to know that your gear placements are good and that the belayer is doing their job well.

Leading a route can take a considerable length of time and your belayer may become restless and inattentive. Both belayer and climber should be happy with how long they expect spend climbing a pitch. Even a momentary loss of concentration by the belayer can result in the climber being dropped.

Belaying a lead climber

Check out the section on double ropes later (p155 for tips on managing two ropes).

Your lead climber's life is in your hands. There is a big difference between belaying someone on a top rope and belaying someone on lead. When you start to belay a lead climber you should have someone with experience close at hand, backing you up. A good belayer will pay constant attention to the climber, watching for movement so they can pay the rope out at the right time. If the climber is out of sight the belayer has to look at the curve of rope going up the crag, and as they see the rope start to straighten or even feel the rope tighten slightly, they need to pay out more rope.

Lead belaying is often a combination of paying out the rope and then taking the rope back in. As the leader places runners above their head (pay out rope), for a moment they are climbing on a mini top rope (take in rope), before they climb past the runner (pay out rope). The belayer can minimise the amount of rope they have to pay out each time by making a step forward or back (just a single step though).

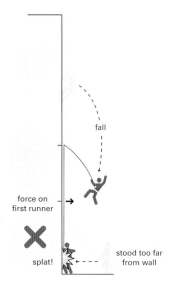

force on first runner

fall

splat!

stood too far from wall

Belay as close to the wall as possible to avoid being pulled into the wall and putting strain on the first runner.

The belayer should be ready to lock-off the rope at any moment, as the climber could fall without warning. A few calls from the leader can be helpful; 'SLACK' means they want some slack paid out, 'WATCH ME' means they want you to be really attentive as they are at a tricky move, 'TAKE' means that they have either fallen off or are about to, or they are exhausted want to rest on the rope and you should lock-off the rope.

The forces involved in a leader fall are far greater than when top rope climbing, so vigilance is needed at all times. If the climber falls from a long way above the runner then there is often an opportunity to take in a quick armful of rope and step backwards to take in some rope and reduce the length of fall, however as soon as the weight starts to come on the rope the rope needs to be locked off. Hold on tight and expect to be lifted off your feet.

Position yourself as close to the bottom of the route as possible. If the climber falls off and you are stood a distance from the base of the cliff you will get dragged across the ground. More importantly, pulling you into the wall may pull the first runner out, potentially leading to a cascade effect pulling each runner out until the top one.

Before the first runner can be clipped it will be necessary to spot the climber on the first moves up from the ground. Check out the next section on safe bouldering for some advice.

Learning to belay a lead climber – It's best to start indoors in a controlled environment. Place some slings over some holds on a low level traverse and practise belaying someone close to the ground.

Practise belaying a leader on a low level traverse. You can use slings around holds to keep your quickdraws in place. Whilst you practise be careful not to 'back-clip', see Clipping Quickdraws from page 139 for an explanation.

Practising in a group of three you can belay the leader simultaneously on a top rope and on a lead rope. If your leader is confident in your belaying, then move on to belaying the leader for real, but have the third person back you up on the dead rope.

climber belayed
on top rope

climber belayed
on lead rope

Simulated lead belaying.

When practising, the leader should only attempt routes that they are confident they can complete without falling. Only after a period of consolidation should you consider moving on to harder climbs. At some point it will be good for the belayer to hold a small lead fall. The leader should be confident in the belayer and the belayer should be backed up by a competent belayer. Practise this on a bolted route, so the leader knows that the runner will hold when they fall.

These steps are also great for the first time leader as it allows them to progressively understand the added risks of lead climbing. The safety of the leader relies on their ability to judge how good the runners are and whether or not they are likely to hold a fall. Judgement comes with instruction and experience.

Lead climbing procedure – Before leaving the ground both the leader and the belayer should check that both have correctly fastened their harnesses, that both are tied into the rope correctly and that the belay plate is threaded correctly and connected to the rope loop made where the belayer has tied in.

Attaching the belay device to the rope loop rather than the harness belay loop adds a small amount of extra stretch into the system when the knot tightens if the climber falls. By tying into the end of the rope it becomes impossible to pay out more rope than you have to the leader.

The leader then climbs the route, placing runners along the way. At the top of the pitch the leader needs to place the first anchor in the belay and clip it as a runner whilst they place at least one other anchor. Only when they have tied into the anchors and adjusted them to get into a good position to look down the pitch they have just climbed should they shout "SAFE" down towards the belayer.

Then the belayer takes the rope out of the belay device and when the rope is free shouts "OFF BELAY".

At crags by the sea or on windy days it becomes very hard to communicate between leader and second. You might have to create your own series of signals based on a number of tugs on the rope. Alternatively small radios have become popular.

This is the cue for the leader to pull the slack rope up hand over hand, until it goes tight on the belayer. When the belayer feels the rope go tight on them they let the leader know by shouting "THAT'S ME".

The leader then places the belayer (now the 'second') on belay, and shouts down "ON BELAY, CLIMB WHEN READY".

Now the second can unclip from their anchor (if they are on a multi-pitch route) and shout up "CLIMBING" as they start to climb, the leader confirms this by shouting down "OK".

Belaying a lead climber: As you pay the rope out, you can add a little extra slack quickly by taking a step closer to the wall.

Factor two falls

Fall factor is the length of fall divided by the length of rope available to absorb the energy of the fall. It's not an exact science but it does help show the kind of force that will be exerted on climber and belayer. Generally the two worst case scenarios are falls when close to the ground, as there is very little rope out, and the fall is often as long as the length of rope (the fall factor is approaching one). Higher up the pitch even on a long fall the amount of rope out to absorb the impact means that the fall factor is often less than a half.

Fall factor diagrams.
Factor 1, factor 0.5,
factor 2 and factor 1.8.

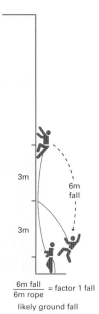
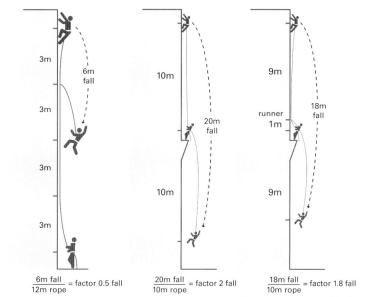

$$\frac{\text{6m fall}}{\text{6m rope}} = \text{factor 1 fall}$$

likely ground fall

$$\frac{\text{6m fall}}{\text{12m rope}} = \text{factor 0.5 fall}$$

$$\frac{\text{20m fall}}{\text{10m rope}} = \text{factor 2 fall}$$

$$\frac{\text{18m fall}}{\text{10m rope}} = \text{factor 1.8 fall}$$

Top runner takes most of the impact,
rather than the belay or belayer

It is only when we leave the stance above the first pitch of a multi-pitch route that we have the potential for a factor two fall. Imagine climbing up four metres from the stance without any gear. The resulting fall will lead to the climber passing the belayer and falling for a total of eight metres, with only four metres of rope out. As well as the highest impact force possible in a climbing fall you are also applying all that force to the belay, and potentially causing catastrophic failure. To avoid this even a runner next to the belay will help reduce the fall factor and protect the belay from the impact.

WARNING – avoid factor two falls from any height (even a few centimetres). Protect the belay with an early runner.

I have witnessed two more consequences of factor two falls. As the leader falls, the live rope goes slack and drops onto the belay. I have seen the belayer attempt to grab the slack live rope, forgetting about holding fast the dead rope. Also I have seen a belayer lock off the dead rope downward beside their hip (correct for a normal lead fall), to watch the leader fall past them where the direction of pull on the anchors changes and the downward grip on the dead rope was no longer the locking off position. The belayer received rope burns to the hands in both situations whilst trying to arrest the leader's fall.

Abseiling

When the climbing becomes too hard or in the face of advancing bad weather or nightfall, abseiling off may be the only option. An abseil may be needed to approach a sea cliff, to retrieve gear or to rescue a stranded climber. The risks posed by most abseils are high but manageable. Over the years there have been several high profile accidents and deaths. These have included anchor failure, equipment failure, rockfall and bad judgement.

A maillon next to a snap gate karabiner: Cheap and strong, great for retreating off routes!

Abseiling into an inaccessible cliff you will need to carry some prussics and know how to use them to ascend the abseil rope you have left in situ, in case you cannot successfully climb out.

Anchor failure has many causes. On some abseil points you will find a web of in-situ slings and cord that have been exposed to harmful ultra-violet from the sun and abuse by other climbers (ropes being pulled through them time and again). Carry your chalk bag on some cord (7mm diameter minimum) and you will be able to cut away the oldest and worst looking tat and replace it with your own. Carrying a small maillon means you can leave it in situ and thread the ropes through that (protecting the cord from rope abrasion).

Anchor failure has from time to time been down to climbers' reluctance to lose their valuable rack. Choosing not to use the best gear you have for the anchor is to value your life at perhaps less than the cost of a couple of wires and a sling.

Don't be cheap when retreating off routes

Once upon a time, two climbers were retreating off a winter route. The first man down had made a belay on three wires. When the second man down reached the ground, he gave the first two of the wires back. The first climber asked "Why did you take them out?" ... He was the director of a well-known gear manufacturer and had a warehouse full of them!

So when retreating –

Don't be cheap.

If you doubt the belay back it up some more.

Check everything twice or more.

A well known American climber fell to his death when his harness' attachment loop failed as he was rappelling of a route because it was worn out. Sadly, he was aware of the condition of his attachment loop and was waiting for a new harness to arrive by post. If the belay loop becomes damaged on a route consider making a new one with a sling around both leg loops and waist belt.

How to rig a belay for an abseil retreat off two wires with a sling and a piece of cord. WARNING: You must abseil and not be lowered off. Rope moving across rope under tension will cut through the rope very quickly.

Other climbers have had accidents when trying to make a retrievable abseil using two ropes of differing lengths and have inadvertently abseiled off one rope. Tying a knot in the end of each rope will prevent this from happening.

Rigging an abseil with a Christmas tree setup; again all the fundamental principles of a belay are employed as it conforms to the IDEAS principles.

Sometimes the approach to the cliff will be by abseil, for which you will leave the abseil rope in position to be retrieved after you have completed the climb. You may need to take a spare rack and some slings to rig it with. If the abseil point is fixed, check all the pegs, bolts, tat or stakes and consider backing them up in one way or another. It is also handy to be able to setup a belay with just the one abseil rope, using a Christmas tree setup. Before you throw the rope over the edge tie a knot in the end in case it doesn't reach the ground, as well as checking that there is no one below you!

Finally in order to make the descent as safe as possible you need to use some form of 'dead-mans handle'. The simplest and best option is a French prussic on the leg loop, as well as possibly extending the belay plate away from you with a sling.

How to tie a French prussic. Using a French prussic as a 'deadman handle' on a abseil. Often the prussic can release itself if it touches the belay plate; as such it is often advisable to extend the belay device away from you with a sling (see below). This gives more friction and stops the prussic releasing unexpectedly.

Setting up for an abseil with an extended sling and direct onto your belay loop.

Pros and cons of extended sling abseil

Belaying off your belay loop puts the dead-mans handle very close to the belay device and the prussic will release if it touches the device.

Extending the belay device reduces the chances of the prussic releasing and creates better friction through the device by changing the angle at which the dead rope leaves the device.

The drawback is that by larks footing the sling to your harness you weaken the sling. Were you to slip standing above the belay (taking a factor two fall onto it) you could snap the sling. If you don't stand above the belay, you shouldn't be able to create enough force to snap the sling.

Never larks foot your extending sling to both your leg and waist loops. This creates a loose larks foot. Test drops of only a couple of metres have melted through Dyneema slings. The larks foot tightens rapidly under load with a lot of friction on a small area. Larks foot your sling to the belay loop only. Never climb above your belay.

RISK: BOULDERING

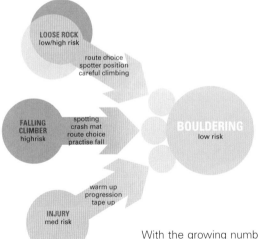

Bouldering is considered by many a low risk pastime. However pushing yourself on highly challenging problems makes the likelihood of a tumble far greater. It could be argued that if you are not failing you aren't trying, falling off is part and parcel of bouldering. Whilst close to the ground the injuries, although rarely life threatening, can be debilitating. A badly twisted ankle will end a day's climbing and may even lay you up for weeks. Simple things will make your session a lot safer; using a bouldering mat(s), good spotting and learning to fall.

With the growing number of bouldering mat owners it is often possible to stack multiple mats to make the landing safer. Stacking mats can lead to hidden pitfalls; be aware of joins in the mats, which can potentially twist ankles. It is possible to double over a bouldering mat to give maximum cushioning, however the edge of the mat is another hazard if you land half-on half-off.

Good spotting takes awareness and experience. Having your hands in your pockets, talking to your mate, is not good spotting. Just like belaying it requires your full attention, as well as some thought as to where to position yourself. A good spot will give the climber the confidence to succeed.

(A) Using chalk to mark the spot where an ankle twisting boulder lies helps you miss them. (B) A well padded-out problem, with numerous stacked and doubled over mats.

When low down we can spot by simply pushing a climber back onto the wall. When working a hard move you can use this to take some 'poundage' off the climber, effectively helping them through the move, until they get the move sufficiently 'dialled'. Being ready to catch or slow a climber down by their bum and armpits can help to reduce impact and help the climber land feet first.

Good spotting comes down to aiding the smooth landing of a falling climber, as trying to catch them is futile. Slowing down a falling climber reduces the force of impact and gives them an extra fraction of a second to adjust their landing. In more extreme falls, simply catching a climbers armpits will help them to land feet first allowing their natural shock absorbers, the legs, to absorb the impact.

The human body is far better at absorbing an impact travelling forward or straight down. Falling backwards our legs struggle to keep us on our feet. So simply pushing a falling climber so they fall forward can help them to help themselves. By accepting the inevitable when you're about to fall and trying to spin round and fall forwards will ensure the safest of landings.

(1) Falling forwards the knees and hips can absorb the impact. (2) Falling backwards the body struggles to absorb the impact as well as travelling forwards, and usually result in landing on your arse.

A fall from a highball is hard to spot, often all you can do is aid the climber to land on their feet moving slightly forwards and direct them to a bouldering mat. In extreme cases when the climber is falling backwards from height, trying to catch their bottom and make a football throw back towards the wall, helps slow the fall and helps the climber land moving forwards.

(A) Spotting a highball arête at Fontainebleau. Catching someone from this height would be dangerous.
(B) Catching their bum as they fall from steep terrain and throwing them forwards will help them to land.

Check out the chapter;
Training: The Basic
Principles page 77 for
more information.

Soft tissue injuries – There is an urge to push ourselves as hard as possible at boulder problems. The strain we place on our fingers, arms and shoulders can be far greater than any other form of climbing. We can injure both the muscles and connective tissue such as tendons, ligaments and the pulleys with the fingers.

Taping up can help prevent this but it is far better to use a thorough warm-up, as well as a slow progression to steeper more fingery problems. After all the human body wasn't designed to support its entire weight on a few fingertips. Whilst the muscle can quickly become capable of this the connective tissue takes longer to develop.

Intensive finger training (in particular campus boards) should be avoided by young people up to the age of 18, as the bone structure in the fingers hasn't fully developed, which can lead to permanent finger deformity (see Training: The Young Climber later in the book).

A fantastic belay on Oberon at Tremadog. The climber has chosen to use snap gates to secure the belay but has arranged the gates so that they are not against the rock.

Warming Up: Body & Mind

(Above) totally pumped!
Warming up can
help prevent this
from happening.

A warm-up will get the heart, lungs, muscles, joints and tendons ready for action. Whilst some people will do a full aerobics style warm-up, some will opt for easy bouldering or climbing. Some climbers will choose to do none. Although this might feel like you will be able to get more climbing in because you have not 'wasted' energy on the warm-up, the opposite is true.

An easy warm-up promotes blood flow through the muscles, dilating the capillaries and actually allowing you to climb harder for longer. Jumping on the hardest route straight away will result in 'flash pump' – your muscles instantly become exhausted because the blood cannot flow effectively through veins and capillaries, as the muscle's contractions restrict the supply.

Warming up – Starts heart and lungs working. Promotes good blood follow through capillaries. Helps tendons prepare for activity by making them more elastic. Helps promote fluid in the joint to increase lubrications. Helps switch the mind to climbing mode.

A good warm-up should last about twenty minutes. It will help to set the scene for your whole session, get you in the right frame of mind and help you to concentrate on skilful climbing.

The pump – Bodybuilders coined the phrase 'the pump' for the swollen feeling and appearance of muscles after a workout. For us it is pertinent to climbing in our anaerobic zone, where the build up of lactic acid makes the muscle less effective. It starts with a dull ache and ends in a complete inability to contract the affected muscles, resulting in failure. If you carry on to failure the muscle will feel solid to touch and you will need at least 15 to 45 minutes rest to recover.

Warming up indoors

Warming up indoors on an easy traversing wall.

Some indoor walls have a gym where you can do an aerobic workout on cycling, running or rowing machines but most do not and you'll need a degree of imagination to warm-up.

At an indoor climbing wall a good warm-up will extend the length of a session, by allowing you to climb harder for longer.

The majority of climbing walls will have some easy top roping for groups; these routes are ideal for warming up on as they will allow you to work your muscles without tiring. You need to operate below the level where you find your arms becoming pumped because of the build up of lactic acid. You should be exercising in an aerobic way. If you do start to become pumped lower off and drop the grade and angle of the routes that you are warming up on. Very easy bouldering on slabs, traverses or juggy routes can offer an alternative.

Throughout the warm-up, how does your body feel; are you finding it intense? If so, make things a easier, the level you warm up at will rarely be too easy. You will be able to feel your body warming up and the blood flowing more freely through the muscles, a raised heart and breathing rate and a glow of light perspiration. Keep going until that feeling is well established (for about twenty minutes).

The warm-up is a great time to introduce some climbing drills that help reinforce technique on this easy terrain. So as part of your warm-up visit some of the exercises we'll cover later on. Exercises like climbing only facing left, then right, being sideways on (zigzagging up the wall), climbing silently, climbing slowly, Climbing one or no handed and climbing like a monkey. All these exercises develop good technique and used during the warm-up will help switch your mind to climbing mode. Doing them every time you go climbing will engrain them in your subconscious and help ensure that you think about efficiency whenever you climb.

Warming up at the wall

Remember climbing during the warm-up can never be too easy!

A warm-up should last for at least twenty minutes.

Consider doing some technique drills.

'Rest – move' warm-up drill, which promotes balance and restful positions.

Warming up at the crag

The walk into a crag helps serves as a warm-up.

At the crag it may be harder to do a thorough warm-up, although sometimes a long walk-in suffices. You may find that by the time you have rigged a top rope or racked up you have already cooled down, so consider doing an easy route as a warm-up. If you have warmed up on the approach wrapping up in an extra layer of clothing once you have arrived at the bottom of the cliff can make a big difference.

If climbing an easy route isn't possible then bouldering up and down the first few moves of a climb several times is a good alternative. This process of going up and down the start of a route can be extended to actually placing gear and coming back down, not only getting warmed up but also getting to know the route and the gear.

Simply walking around the bottom of the crag, moving and flexing your arms and hands as well as jogging on the spot will all help to get the heart and lungs into gear. Whatever you do, any form of warm-up will help you climb better and fight off the pump.

Warming up at the crag

The walk-in can be part of the warm-up.

Start on an easy route or boulder up and down the start of the route.

Boulder around the base of the crag.

Use an easy route or small boulder to work on technique.

STRETCHING

Having warmed up you should move onto some stretching exercises. Warmed up you are far less likely to injure yourself by pulling a muscle whilst stretching. Stretching before a climb shouldn't necessarily be about holding positions that stretch individual muscles, warm-up exercises that make you work through a your range of movement, like arm windmills, leg sprints and even engaging in a quick game of hacky sack may be better.

Bridging often requires a high degree of flexibility. Stretching it out on Jack of Shadows E4 Colossus Wall.

Warm up to stretch, don't stretch to warm up!

To get the most out of your stretching you shouldn't bounce in the stretch, instead just go gradually as far as is comfortable and hold that position for at least ten seconds. If you bounce, the muscles and tendons stretch like an elastic band and unless you hold the position for long enough they will not elongate. As your flexibility improves with regular stretching, you will be able to hold the stretches for longer.

Training flexibility – Stretching muscles regularly will increase their useful range of movement. Sometimes we are forced into brutal geometries, wide bridging or contorted positions. Without flexibility it will be hard to use your muscles at the limit of your mobility.

As well as stretching before your session after a good warm-up, greater improvements can be made by taking time to stretch in your daily routine. Yoga or Pilates will aid flexibility as well as muscle tone and core strength. When you are stretching to train flexibility, hold your stretch for at least twenty seconds and you should be able to build up to holding them for a minute.

Your sports physiotherapist may offer PNF (Propriorceptor neuromuscular facilitation) stretching. This is an advanced form of stretching that involves muscle contraction and resistance, which requires expert supervision to avoid injury. A physiotherapist can measure your gains in flexibility as well as offer advice and treatment on the general aches and pains of climbing.

As a lazy warm-up for stretching sessions at home you can take a hot shower or bath.

It is useful to use a systematic approach to your stretches, to ensure that all the major muscle groups are included, starting at the head and working down to the toes or vice versa.

More important is to stretch after climbing too. Your climbing-specific muscles will be warmed up, so it's a great opportunity to stretch these in particular.

Stretching myths

Stretching reduces strength – True, but only by 2–5% immediately after stretching. The effect can last for up to one hour. It might conceivably affect you on a very hard redpoint, if you stretch just before you climb, but you are unlikely to ever notice the effect.

Stretching increases strength – True, seemingly contradictory to the above. It is true that regular stretching can result in 2–5% increase in muscle strength.

Stretching helps to prevent injuries – Debatable. Several large studies of military groups has shown no overall benefit. But the injuries recorded included fractures, something you're more likely to get soldiering than climbing and unlikely to be helped by stretching. In general it seems that stretching before exercise has little effect, but regular stretching (separate to exercise) can reduce soft tissue injury.

Warming up reduces injury – True. A small increase in muscle temperature has been shown to reduce the likelihood of muscle tears.

Static vs dynamic stretching – Debatable. There is little evidence on this matter. Anecdotally, dynamic stretching (lunges, kicks, muscle resistance and whatnot) can reduce the chance of injury. This needs to be specific to your climbing, working legs, shoulders and arms. But climbing often requires you to hold static stretches. Regularly training static stretches will increase your range of movement.

Stretches

1. When stretching the neck go from side to side, then up and down. Never rotate as there is a small risk of trapping a nerve.

Four ways to stretch the shoulder, each one helps isolate different parts of the complex muscular system. **2.** Across the neck. **3.** Behind the head. **4.** Link arms behind back. **5.** Against the wall.

Stretching out the various muscles and tendons in the arms, hands, fingers and thumbs. **6.** A simple forearm stretch, which can be reversed, pulling back on the fingertips to stretch the whole forearm. **7.** Rotating forearm stretch.

Stretching the sides of the body and mobilising the back. **8.** Run a hand down one leg and concentrate on not leaning over forwards or back. **9.** This can be developed by putting an arm over your head.

Stretching the back, bottom and hamstring. **10.** Start with your legs about shoulder width apart and reach as far down with both hands towards one foot and then the other. Then reach for the floor. Do not bounce. **11.** Then bring your feet together and reach as far down your legs as you can. **12.** Stretch the hamstring by putting one foot in front of the other and turn the back foot out to the side. Keep the front leg straight and lift the toes, whilst slumping down on the back foot.

13. Sit on the floor and spread your legs so you feel the groin start to stretch but so they are still straight, then reach out first for your left foot and hold for 10 seconds. Then reach over to your right foot and then reach out to the floor in front. **14.** Sit on the floor and bring the base of your feet as close to your groin as comfortable, the apply some added pressure from the hands/elbows down on the knees, hold for 10 second and then repeat again.

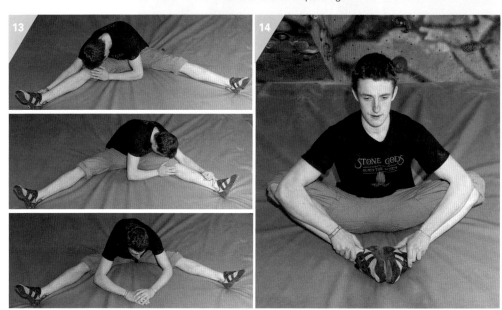

15. Stretching the thigh. Stand on one foot, you may wish to place a hand against a wall for support. Grab the foot of the free leg and pull it towards the buttock whilst pulling the knees together and pushing your hips forwards. **16.** Stretching calf muscle. Using a wall or small boulder, place your toes 10 to 20 cm up the wall and place your heel on the ground. With a straight leg move into the wall to develop the stretch. **17.** Place your foot on a hold about waist height, and move your hips as close to the wall as possible.

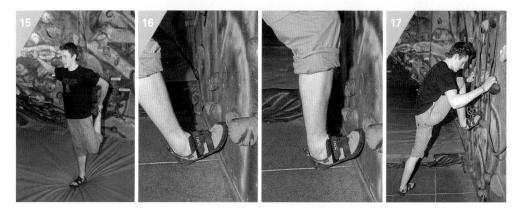

18. Stretching your glutes. Lie of the floor and cross one foot over the opposite knee. Then slowly raise the knee until you feel the stretch.

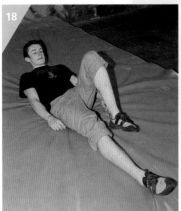

EXERCISE YOUR MIND

After you have warmed up and stretched some coordination exercises will focus your concentration on kinaesthesia (your sense of movement), proprioception (sense of space) and balance. We can effectively turn on the part of the brain that we use for learning and acquiring new skills.

In the long term, these types of exercises can become second nature, it is in the context of the learning to learn that these exercises will benefit you for the first few sessions that you use this book.

Body and mind exercises

Balance on one foot and move upper body and other limb to counter balance each other.

Rub tummy, pat head whilst balancing on one foot. Put the other foot forwards, left, right and back.

Rotate arms in opposite directions whilst walking around then change your direction of travel.

Basic juggling; then move to see if you can do it on one leg?

Rotate your right foot in a clockwise direction and then with your right hand write a number six in the air.

Run on the spot with your legs going in slow motion and your arms as fast as possible and vice versa.

(A) Rubbing tummy and patting head whilst standing on one foot. Try shifting your balance by moving the free leg and upper body. (B) One legged crouch. Go down as far as you feel comfortable with, as this exercise causes great strain on the knee. Then try and stand back up.

The Basics: Footwork & Balance

Most important to efficient climbing is proper footwork that takes the strain off your hands. Wes Hunter balances along the ripple on Poetry Pink.

Imagine two identical twin climbers with equal strength, one uses their feet and body position well, the other doesn't. The twin who uses their feet and body more effectively will be a far better climber. Rather than stumble upon good technique there are some essential building blocks which you can drill into your climbing. So here are some exercises that you can repeat and test on different climbing surfaces.

So that they can be repeated until they become second nature, many of the exercises need to be practised on easy terrain. And by keeping the climbing simple we can gauge which techniques feel easier. For footwork exercises, small slabby boulders can be very useful as hands are superfluous. Otherwise start them on easy top-roped routes.

Smearing and edging

Although these exercises appear as a progression, parts of them should and can be used as part of a warm-up or during climbing and re-visited so you can work on areas of your technique.

'Edging' is standing on a small edge or a tiny ledge. 'Smearing' is when the rock is featureless so we smear as much of the surface of our boot against the rock as possible and use the friction of the boot rubber to hold our foot in place.

Smearing and edging exercise – On a small and very gently inclined boulder, stand on an edge and then on a smear. Then experiment with different parts of the boot. Inside and outside edges, heel and the toe.

Try using smaller edges and poorer smears on steeper rock. What is the limit of the rock type you are on? Are other rock types different? If so, how? Which is easier, smearing or edging? Which is easier inside/outside edge, heel or toe? Could you put them in order of strain on the calf muscles? Over time you will build up the foot strength to stand on smaller and smaller edges, as well as an appreciation of what is possible to smear on different rock types.

Now climb up a gently inclined boulder trying to utilise first edges, then smears and finally both in ascent and descent.

(A) Edging. (B) Smearing.

Using the (C) heel, (D) inside edge of boot, (E) outside edge, and (F) toe.

Edging tips

Don't drop the heel.

Try and keep the ankle at 90 degrees.

Smearing tips

Drop the heel.

Try and get as much rubber on the base of the foot in contact as possible.

Stepping up

At times deliberate experimentation with bad technique can reinforce your idea of good technique.

Stepping up exercises – Walk up a gently inclined slab boulder taking first giant steps and then tiny steps. Which feels the easiest?

Try facing directly up the slab and climbing up and then try facing only right and then only left, at times it will feel quite unnatural as you have to backstep. After that try to link facing left and right by walking up in a series of zigzags pivoting around at the end of each zig. During this exercise you will need to stand on the inside edge of one foot and the outside of the other. Which one required less effort from your leg muscles?

Climbing up facing only right, back stepping the left leg. Side-on the calf is under less strain and it is easier to balance.

If you are climbing side-on to the rock, you will tend to move diagonally, which means you will have to zigzag up the rock. Pivot around your toes to change direction.

Being side-on and using the edge of the foot rather than the toe instantly reduces the leverage on your calf muscle. The distance between your heel and the point of contact is reduced. Also your centre of gravity also comes closer to the wall, reducing the weight on your arms.

By the end of these exercises you will have realised that as well as edging rock shoes can also smear the rock where there are no footholds (although this becomes more difficult on steeper rock). Also, giant steps are less efficient than small ones and being side-on is less strenuous and more stable.

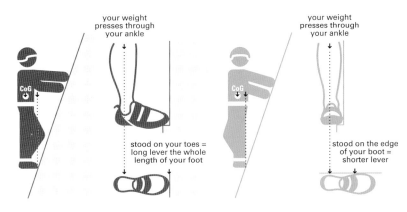

your weight presses through your ankle

CoG

stood on your toes = long lever the whole length of your foot

your weight presses through your ankle

CoG

stood on the edge of your boot = shorter lever

Standing sideways on a foothold can bring your centre of gravity (CoG) closer to the wall. It can also decrease the distance between your ankle and your point of contact with the wall. Standing on tip toes creates a lot of leverage through your ankle and puts a lot of strain on your calf muscle. Less distance equals less leverage equals more efficient footwork.

The next step is to move onto more realistic climbing terrain, either on slabby boulders, top ropes or seconding routes. Over time these tricks will become second nature.

Stepping up exercise 2 – Just like the previous exercise, but this time on a easy slab climb that requires you to use your hands for balance. Face right so that you are looking along the wall, and climb the route keeping your shoulders perpendicular to the wall. You will be forced to back step onto holds. Repeat this facing to the left.

Now climb the same route, facing sideways, but this time concentrate on facing one way and simply walking forwards up the climb until you run out of foot holds. Then pivot round to face the other direction, zig-zagging up the route.

Then; don't allow the outside arm to touch the rock, pretend you are taking a phone call and as you pivot round change which ear you have to the phone. Rely entirely on the inside arm for balance. This will put you in a more natural body position; at first it may seem more difficult.

This can be progressed further still on many easier slabs to either no handed or just using the palm of your hand for balance.

Backstepping onto a foot hold. The centre of gravity (belly button) travels from over the front foot to the back foot.

(A) Side-on climbing using both hands. (B) Only the inside hand (keeps the body sideways to the rock). (C) With no hands (you'll realise that the hands aren't the most important connection to the rock).

Side-on tips

Concentrate on facing at 90° to the rock face.

You will almost be walking up the slab.

Find a point of balance in between moving and stop, use this to move your hands.

At times you will need to backstep.

Foot matching and swapping

You may find yourself in a position where you appear to have your feet in the wrong position for the next move. Rather than making the next move an awkward one it is often possible to shift your feet around in one of three ways, the foot dance, foot match or foot swap – changing the foot that is stood on a crucial hold.

A foot dance using another nearby foothold to swap feet. The left foot ends up where the right foot began.

The foot dance requires three footholds to choose from and making a series of moves until you manage to get the other foot on the foothold you want.

(Right) think ahead to place your foot to allow the other room to share the foothold and you may be able to 'match' both feet onto the single hold.

The foot swap is good when your foothold is too small to match on and there are no other options. Place your second foot directly above the foot you want to replace, get the big toe right above the other, and hop. During the hop remove the lower foot and the top foot should drop right onto the hold. Alternatively you can foot swap by twisting the first foot across the hold to make room for the second. Once the second foot is in place you can likewise twist it over the hold to get better contact.

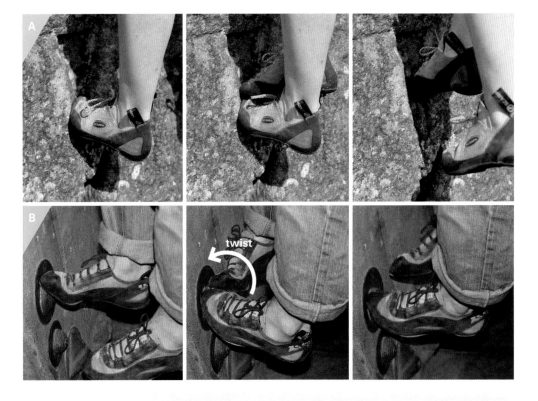

Foot swaps: (A) Hopping one foot out and the other in. (B) by twisting the first foot to accommodate the second.

Foot swapping exercise – On a low traverse or warm-up route make foot swaps on every move; remember to try the foot dance, foot match and foot swap. As you get more confidence start making more and more tenuous foot swaps, and eventually you will have an idea of how small a foot hold you can do this on.

Stepping up drills – The following exercises should be carried out on an easy top rope route. They require you to climb in different styles. Keep in mind the techniques you want to work on/experiment with.

Slowly – Climbing slowly will help you feel the transfer of weight from one foot to the next. As you rock slowly from onto the other foot you should also feel the weight transferred between your hands. Repeat this exercise; this time relax your fingers. You might find that you can let go at times on slabby routes. Great as part of a warm-up.

Silently – To be silent you need to move precisely. The chances are you will look at your feet a lot more and exercise foot eye coordination as well as controlled weight transfer from foot to foot.

Like a monkey – How do monkeys climb? They have grasping feet and usually get their feet really high and pull up onto them. Imagine your feet are hands, don't just put your foot on a high hold, try and grab it with your toes inside your rock shoes. Grabbing the hold with you toes helps to make a more secure foothold and you may be able to use your leg as a pulling limb, not just a pushing one.

Aggressively – Imagine someone being aggressive; they are usually tense and their movement overly powerful. Try climbing like this and see how it compares! This aggressive style is similar in many ways to what happens to us when we get scared, our bodies tense up and we start to waste vital energy.

Quickly – Climb a route as quickly as you can. This may not make you more efficient, but it will give you an indication of how your subconscious climbing is coming along. Over time you may find that you can climb harder and harder routes in this way or that the speed with which you climb a particular grade has increased. Make sure the belayer can keep up!

Fluidly – Make your movements flow one into the next. Switching your balance and body position all the time. This can help your spatial awareness.

Blindfolded – You are reliant on your sense of balance and spatial awareness. Concentrate on the feeling of movement. Remember to find positions that are in balance and relaxed. Rather than using a blindfold, it may be safer to just close you eyes, so you can open them if you are going to fall.

Hands below shoulders – Climb without reaching above your shoulders. This will make you work your feet and establish positions of balance when moving your hands.

Sideways – Use all the sideways climbing movements (two handed, one handed, no handed, facing left, facing right, zig-zagging) as part of this series of drills for promoting good technique.

Precise footwork

The lazy climber doesn't shuffle around. Place your feet where they need to be, first time, every time. There are three easy exercises that can develop your awareness of using your feet to your best advantage.

Look before placing – This is a simple exercise that can be done on any traverse indoors or out, and should be continued throughout your climbing. To start with find a easy traverse, look at the foot holds and identify the best place to put either foot on the hold. Then climb the traverse and concentrate on placing your feet exactly how you envisaged.

Accuracy exercise – Make a selection of targets on a wall (gaffa tape squares with a dot or a simple chalk dot). Stand away from the wall and try to place the tip of you toe straight onto the target. The slower the better, as there is often a trade-off between speed and accuracy. Once you have done this a few times with both left and right feet, change position and try again. Also try standing with your toes touching the wall then reach out with one leg to either side (try crossing in front of the leg you are standing on too). Now stand on the wall and try the same exercise from a climbing position.

(A) Developing foot accuracy using targets.
(B) Balancing a cork on a foothold reduces the target area and demands careful footwork not to knock it off.

Cork traverse – Go back to your easy traverse and see if you can balance a selection of corks on the biggest footholds. Climb the traverse again, trying not to knock the corks from the holds. Reverse the route, add more corks or try a different traverse to vary your practice.

The Basics: Handholds & Body Position

As well as good foot work you also need to be able to hang on with your hands!

The lazy climber knows that the hands and arms are the smallest and weakest muscle group used in climbing; it's vital to save as much energy as possible when we use them by using holds as effectively as we can.

Stay as relaxed as you can. The more relaxed in mind the more relaxed your grip. It is no coincidence that a scared climber is often described as being 'gripped'. As anxiety increases so does your grip on whatever you can hold on to. Often even though you are in a position that when relaxed your hands might just be holding you in balance, you will be hanging on like your life depended on it.

You can often trick your brain into feeling more comfortable by relaxing your arms, as the realisation dawns that you aren't in as bad a position as you thought.

To overcome this we need to learn not only how to compose ourselves, but also to know what it feels like to be relaxed, so during any of these exercises rate your grip on a scale of 1 to 5.

1 Very light – finger tips just touching the holds

2 Light – holding a cup of tea

3 Medium – a firm hand shake

4 Hard – holding a heavy bag

5 Very hard – you are totally maxed out.

Why do we overgrip? One theory is that as we are overcome by a growing anxiety, we compensate for our reduced cognitive ability by increasing the effort we put into a task.

Try slowing your breathing down (a dose of adrenaline does exactly the opposite). By slowing everything down you are counteracting the natural fight or flight response your body has to stressful or fearful situations.

This is the start of the mental head game of climbing, and there are many theories as to how best to mentally prepare. This will be covered more fully in a later chapter.

Handhold tips

During all exercises relax your arms as much as possible.

Slow your breathing, in through the nose out through the mouth.

Make sure you have hold of the best part of the hold (the 'sweet spot'). Search out the area around the hand hold, an inch to the left or the right the hold might be better.

Keep your arms as straight as possible (so as to hang on your skeletal structure, rather than straining your biceps and shoulders).

Try different foot and body positions, to move your centre of gravity.

WARNING – when climbing it is important to remove rings from fingers; failure to do so has lead to people effectively skinning their own fingers! If you look up 'degloving injuries' be warned, they are gruesome.

CRIMPS

A crimp is the most instinctive way to grab a handhold (if you have ever climbed over a brick wall for example). There are three different types of crimp, the full crimp, half crimp and open handed crimp, all of which enable us to cling onto the tiniest of edges.

Three different ways to hold an edge. (1) The open crimp. (2) The half crimp. (3) The full crimp.

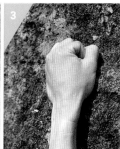

Crimp exercise – Climb using only full crimps, then half and then open. Are some holds easier to hang with one of the three crimps? Try and make a move off the smallest crimp you can when open handed, half crimped and full crimped. Is there a difference?

Crimping tips

In the full crimp, you reinforce the fingers by locking your thumb over the top of the index finger.

Crimps are quite aggressive. It is easy to injure fingers, because our muscles grow stronger more quickly than the tendons, ligaments and pulleys in our fingers.

The bone, tendons, ligaments and pulleys of the hand and fingers can all be injured when climbing.

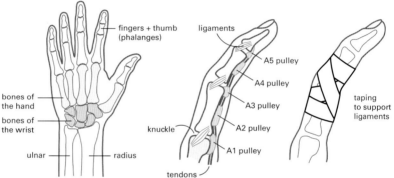

fingers + thumb (phalanges)
ligaments
bones of the hand
bones of the wrist
ulnar
radius
knuckle
tendons
A5 pulley
A4 pulley
A3 pulley
A2 pulley
A1 pulley
taping to support ligaments

FINGER INJURY AVOIDANCE – The hands are prone to injury. We ask the smallest parts in our skeleton to support nearly all of our weight. At first our fingers are not conditioned to deal with these loads. After years of training the potential for injury is still high. The best way to avoid injury is to be aware of this and build up slowly to more 'fingery' boulder problems. To start with climb on fingery holds (a hold that only reaches the first joint, about 10mm) on vertical walls only, as this will limit the amount of force you can apply to the fingers. Over weeks, months and years slowly increase the angle of wall that you use with fingery holds. Listen to your body, a slight twinge or any acute pain is a precursor to injury, so rest your hands and fingers.

Under the age of eighteen bones are not yet fully grown. There is a record of permanent finger deformity among elite junior climbers (see p209).

A good warm-up will help prevent injury but there is no way to avoid tremendous strain on the fingers. On particularly hard ascents you might strap your fingers up with zinc oxide tape to support the soft tissue. Taping up every time can be counter-productive as it doesn't allow your soft tissue to develop and strengthen as you climb.

(1) taping up to support A1/A2 pulleys.

(2) the tape has been over tightened, as it is restricting the blood supply.

(3) taping to support the A3/A4/A5 pulleys.

(4) using a thin piece of tape to make a cross support for the middle ligaments of the finger.

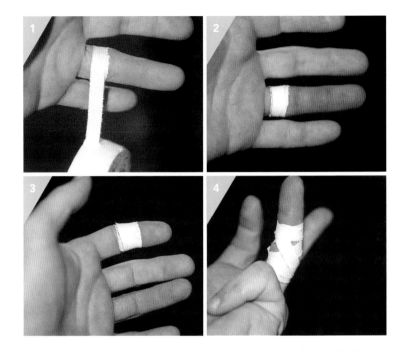

Taping up tips

When taping up the fingers you need to insure that the tape is tight enough to give support but not too tight so that the blood flow is restricted.

CUPPING

A great technique for holding onto small spikes, it often can be used as it uses slightly different muscles to the crimp or sloper, as it relies more on the little finger and ring finger.

Cupping the hold. Mould your hand to fit round the shape of the hold.

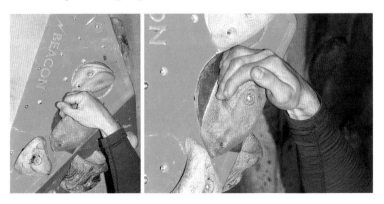

SLOPERS

A sloper; hanging them is an art in itself. Note the low body position and straight arm.

For many a sloper is the worst type of hold. It's the equivalent of the foot 'smear', we have to use friction to enable us to hang on. On these, the most marginal of hand holds, hanging on often relies on us using not only hand strength but body position as well.

Sloper exercises – Find a sloper and experiment with different hand positions on the hold, whilst standing on the ground and try to find a 'sweet spot'.

Now try hanging onto the sloper and experiment with different body and foot positions, like having your shoulder above and below the sloper, and then to the right and left. What feels easier, above or below? Is being in line easier to hang than having your body to the side? Try the exercise for both hands, when holding on with the right hand where is the best body position? What about the left hand?

Now traverse and climb up and down on slopers and ask yourself the same questions.

Sloper tips

Stay low.

Keep your arms straight.

When moving on slopers, try pivoting around your shoulders with your arms straight.

PINCHES & SPRAGS

The opposable thumb is what sets us apart from most of the animal kingdom. It has given us amazing dexterity and arguably a foot up the evolutionary ladder, and for most it is an under used weapon in climbing.

It can be used to reinforce a crimp; by hooking over the index finger, change a hideous sloper into a satisfying pinch, and a lot more besides. The fact is that many people just pull down on holds, and don't really think of improving their grip. Look at and feel the hold before you take the final grip of it and usually you will find a better grasp than a simple crimp, often by finding a way to pinch and bringing the thumb into play (especially useful indoors as bolt on holds often allow you to pinch them).

(1+2) Whilst crimping a small hold in a corner or crack will be fine, pushing against the wall with the thumb (a sprag) helps makes the hold a lot more secure. (3) Pinching a sloping hold.

Thumb exercises – Climb up on either crimps or slopers on an indoor wall, without using your thumb. Repeat the exercise using your thumbs to try and pinch the holds. Which approach feels more secure?

Climb a new problem but this time look at each hold before you go to grasp it, then try and loosely grip it in three different ways, before finally committing to grip it in the best orientation you can find.

Spragging exercises – Now try spragging a sidepull in a corner and moving up on the hold. Repeat the problem just crimping the hold. Which felt easier on the arms? Which required more lay backing to hold? Which felt more secure?

JAMMING

Hand jamming up Brant Direct, Llanberis Pass.

Jamming is a dying art. Climbing walls encourage you to learn to use crimps and slopers but not how to jam; for most new climbers this is an outmoded skill. However, done well a jam is easier to hold than the biggest of jugs.

The methods for an effective jam are as extensive as the variety of cracks that it is possible to climb, from the tightest of finger cracks to the gnarliest of off-widths. Jamming involves wedging part or parts of your body into a crack or fissure. This can be painful and uncomfortable

to start with so you may wish to consider taping up your hands or fingers, your tolerance of the pain will develop. Typically the harder you apply your jam the less likely your hands or fingers are to slip. The slippage is more painful than the jam.

Finger jamming

The thinnest of cracks can be jammed with the smallest tool you have – your fingers. The width that you can jam easily depends on the thickness of your fingers, thinner cracks are better suited to thinner fingers.

Finger jamming exercises – Find a crack you can just fit your fingers in, with the little finger at the top and thumb at the bottom. Then twist the hand down, this should lock the finger into the crack, most commonly onto one of the finger joints.

At first just pull down on the lock with increasing force then, when happy, step off the ground and finally make a move up on the jam. If it is a continuous crack can you make a series of jams up the crack?

Finger jamming relies on your fingers being wider in one orientation than the other. 1. Place them in the crack vertically 2. Then twist them to lock.

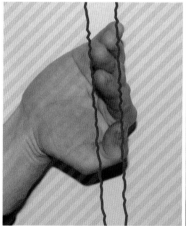
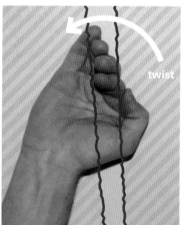

twist

Finger jamming tips

Remember to try both hands.

Cracks are very rarely totally uniform, so try and find a natural tapering, the sort of wedge-shaped space in a crack that might take a wire for protection.

Different fingers and joints have different widths.

Ring-locks

These are good in cracks between fingers and hand width, but are difficult and painful even when mastered. Essential you are using your thumb and index finger to make a wedge. The thumb is reasonably passive and the index finger is used to develop the lock by pulling down across the thumb.

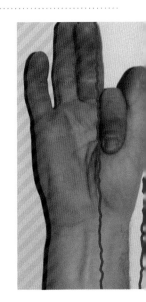

The ring-lock, a difficult jam to master. The lock is developed by pulling down on the index finger.

Ring-lock exercise – Put your thumb and index finger in a crack where they just fit, with the first joint of the index finger running along the thumb, pull the joint down the thumb until it locks. This jam is very dependent on the width of the crack and has very little width tolerance but requires a high tolerance to pain.

Ring-lock tips

Try both hands.

Find a natural tapering in the crack. This form of jamming has very little tolerance to width of the crack.

Ring-locks are painful.

Off-hands

Too wide for fingers to adequately jam in the crack but too small for a satisfying hand-jam. Generally awkward and insecure and the size of crack is totally dependent on your hand and finger size. What is off-hands for you may well be fingers or hands for someone else.

Off-hands exercise – Place your hand into the crack, either thumb up or down, as far as it will go (to be off-hands it will usually stop at the knuckles). Twist your hand sideways and push out inside the crack with the fingers and hope that it stays put. Sometimes using your thumb in opposition to your fingers can help.

Another off-hands method of jamming is to put your index finger and thumb as far into the crack as possible and then try and bring them together until the jam locks.

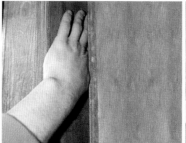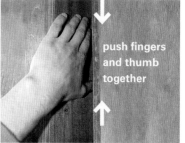

push fingers
and thumb
together

Like all these exercises try both hands, thumbs up and down, and gradually build up to making a move off the jam.

Hand-jams

Hand-jams are the best of the jams that we can use, a good one is better than a jug and a hand will fit a wide variety of cracks. They can be used in different ways by orientating the thumb to be up or down in the crack. Thumbs up allows you to move up easily on a jam as well as rest, whilst thumbs down allows you to reach up as far as possible to a good jam.

To develop a hand-jam, place your hand in a crack either thumbs up or down, and then by trying to touch your little finger with your thumb you will make your hand wider, and jam your hand in place.

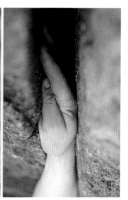

Hand-jamming exercises – Put your hand in a crack, with the thumb pointing up. Try to touch your little finger with your thumb and press your fingers against the inside of the crack.

Pull on the jam to get a feel for it before stepping off the ground; when happy move up on the hand-jam. If the crack is continuous try making a series of moves upward. Alternate left and right hands.

Try the exercise again but with the thumb pointing down. Which is easier to move up further on? Try moving up with both thumbs up then both thumbs down and then with the top hand thumb pointing down, bottom hand thumb point up. Which is easier to move up?

Try moving up a hand-jamming crack by making as many jams as possible, then by making as few jams as possible.

Climb the crack again, first hand over hand, then try leading with the same hand every time and bringing the bottom hand to just below the top before moving the top hand up again.

Hand-jamming tips

Try both hands.

Find a natural tapering in the crack.

Keep your arms as straight as possible and pivot around your shoulders.

Remember you can hand-jam thumbs up and thumbs down.

A hand-jamming crack often allows bomber foot jams in the same crack.

Often the harder you try to jam the less painful they are as your hand will not slip.

Ben Bransby prepares with his 'Yosemite glove', about to tackle the Yosemite jamming classic The Good Book, You can tape up for a hand-jamming crack, or if a crack is likely to be rough like gritstone or granite. You can remove the glove and reuse it, by cutting the wrist loop.

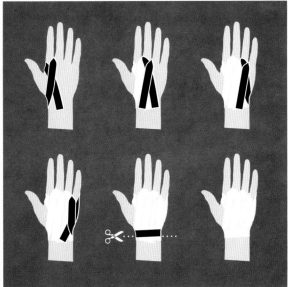

Fist jams

For most people, a fist-jam is just above the width that it is possible to hand jam. That width is totally dependent on the width of your hand. So whilst at times a fist-jam might feel secure, most of the time they will feel quite tenuous and at times painful to maintain.

Fist-jamming exercise – Find a suitable crack and place your hand in with the palm facing down. If the crack is the right width by making a fist, you should be able to jam the fist in place. Try pulling on the jam, then try moving up on it. Try a fist-jam by placing the fist in the crack palm facing up.

Fist-jamming tips

Look for natural taperings in the crack.

Try both hands.

Experiment with different widths.

Pain tolerance is essential for this particular technique.

Keep the arm as straight as possible.

Pivot around the shoulder.

Off-width jams

The mere word instils dread in many. 'Off-width' means all the sizes that our fingers, hands and fist don't quite fit, it means that we have to improvise with the rest of our bodies. It is possible to have an 'off-hands crack', but most people, when referring to 'off-width', mean those cracks between a fist-jam and a chimney.

By burying one shoulder and arm deep into the crack, you can bend the arm at the elbow and make a reasonable jam between the palm of the hand and the upper arm.

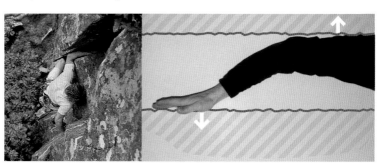

The arm-bar or 'chicken wing' is a great technique. Place your elbow upwards in the crack and let the fingers of your hand point down. As your weight pulls down on the elbow, the arm pivots round the palm and locks tightly in place.

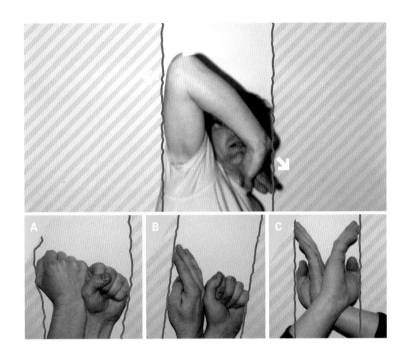

Stacked jams come in a variety of forms, all require good foot-locks and generally a great deal of shuffling around to make upwards progress. The difficulty comes when you need to release a hand. (A) fist to fist, (B) hand to fist and (C) hand to hand.

Spatial and body awareness are needed to decide which brace to 'unlock' before you move on. Your knees become an essential tool, as do your arms and shoulders. Some useful things to try are arm-locks, arm-bars, shoulder-wedges, stacked jams, knee-locks, foot-locks and foot-jams (whilst we're talking about handholds 'off-width' is no holds barred climbing, your whole body is needed).

By placing a knee into a crack whilst the leg is straight, and then bending the knee, it is possible to jam the knee in place.

Foot-jams and locks can provide a solid foundation when climbing cracks. To jam the foot, place the foot in on its side and then twist. The foot-lock helps when you are on wider cracks, greater than the width of your foot. Here you try and brace the foot between heal and toe on either wall of the crack.

Off-width exercise – Find an off-width slot or other horror show, then rig a top rope and experiment. It is often easy to rest in a jammed position but is very strenuous to move between positions. Most off-width climbing is a form of wedging freestyle, some grow to love it.

Off-width tips

Whilst stacked jams are more secure than arm and shoulder-locks, they require some form of lower limb lock to allow you to make upwards progress. Otherwise you can't release them.

Off-widths are like a battle ground, you have to fight for victory.

When approaching an off-width, you need to decide which way to face, left or right side into the crack, it is nearly impossible to change sides once you have started.

ORIENTATION

A straight pull is easier to hold, but harder to move up a long way on as it needs to be locked off by your waist.

A sidepull is harder to hold initially, but if you turn and face it and stand to one side, they are easier to hold nearer your waist as you lay away off it. With a straight arm your feet can do most of the work.

An undercut is hard to hold above your shoulder but as you move up, the easier it becomes, allowing you to reach further.

All these holds and jams come in a variety of orientations from sidepulls to undercuts and straight down pulls. Side pulls and undercuts, whilst often harder to hold, can allow greater range of movement with your other limbs.

Hold orientation exercise – Find a good crimp on a vertical wall, pull up on it, and reach with your free hand to touch the wall as high as you can. Experiment with moving your feet as high as possible and using different body positions.

Find a similar sized crimp which is a sidepull. Experiment with moving your feet as high as possible and using different body positions to reach as high as you can with your free hand.

Then find a similar sized crimp which is an undercut. Experiment with moving your feet as high as possible and using different body positions to reach as high as you can with your free hand. Which allowed you to reach the farthest? How easy was each reach?

On a vertical wall hold on with a straight down pull, sidepull and undercut, with each grip try holding it in three places, above your shoulder, level with your shoulder and below your shoulder. Are the different holds easier or harder to hold at the different levels?

Experiment with different foot and body positions as well as with your left and right hand. Repeat the exercise with the three orientations again, facing right, left and straight onto the wall. Does facing one direction make it easier to hold the position and reach further. Is there a relationship between the way you face and whether you are using your right or left hand?

Finally try using the three orientations of handholds in line with the centre of your body, near your shoulder and out to the side. Which was easier, which allowed you to reach further?

Hold orientation tips

Remember the earlier exercise of being sideways.

Pivot around the shoulders.

Keep your arms straight and push with the legs.

Undercuts are hard to hold above the waist
but become easier once below.

Sidepulls are a good compromise between the distance that you can
reach off an undercut and the ease of holding a straight down pull.

FLAGGING

Using your legs and feet as a counterweight can often help balance between holds of an awkward orientation, or help stretch that little bit further
by smearing against an imaginary hold. 'Flagging' is using whichever leg
you are not standing on as a counter balance, by extending that leg to one
side and perhaps smearing against the wall as well.

You might use an inner and outer flag, depending on whether you put the
leg you are counterbalancing with between the leg stood on the hold and
the wall (inner flag), or put the counterbalancing leg outside the leg stood
on the hold (outer flag).

(A) Inside flagging
sequence and
(B) outside flagging.

Flagging exercise – Grasp a hold and reach out for a hold to the side, as you reach use your free leg as a counterbalance to your upper body. Then try the same reach without counterbalancing. Which feels easier?

Find positions that force you to make an inner or outer flag, see how it feels to reach up for holds at various times on an imaginary clock from 10 o'clock through to 2 o'clock. Do this both left and right handed, try forcing yourself to cross through, as well.

As you practise this reaching for holds, concentrate on your counterbalancing leg, can you make it more steady by pushing the hanging foot onto imaginary holds (smearing the wall)?

Flagging tips

Use the free limb as a counterbalance.

Try inner and outer flags.

Try smearing with the free foot as well as flagging.

Push the flagging foot into the wall to counteract the barn door effect.

Basic Hands-off Rests

Finding a relaxed and restful position to place a runner at Subluminal, Swanage.

As a lazy climber you should plan to move between positions of rest and respite as you move up. These positions may not always be obvious but there are some simple techniques which you can call upon to succeed when at your limit.

When you find a rest you need to be able to 'shake out' the lactic acid that has built up in your arms and legs, to recover your strength. Blood is pumped into the muscles by the heart, but it is contractions in the muscles that help pump the de-oxygenated blood through the veins back to the heart. Continually tense muscles put pressure on the veins and capillaries shutting down new blood entering and the used blood leaving.

The are several schools of thought on how to shake out. Shaking your hands and moving your fingers is the simplest. Holding your arms above your head, gravity may help in the process. However, gravity will be working against the blood flowing up into the muscle, so alternate between above the shoulder and below. Stretching and massaging the muscles in the forearms may also help blood flow. If the rest is a good one, take a break to use all these methods. If you don't feel recovered then you won't be, I have known climbers rest for over an hour whilst halfway up a pitch.

LEDGE REST

The simplest of hands-off rests; a ledge.

Simple enough, you can stand in balance or sit down on a ledge to regain your composure before heading off again. Use them as often as you can. Standing sideways can help rest your calf muscles as well as your arms. You can shake out your calf muscle in a similar way to your forearms, by moving your foot up and down, shaking your lower leg from the knee, rotating your ankle and wiggling your toes.

SLAB REST

The slab is another easy way to get both hands off. Try resting with one or both knees against the rock, to make the whole position more stable and give your hands a break. By standing sideways on your footholds you rest your calf muscles too. Rest your arms for too long stood facing the rock on a slab and you will put more strain your calf muscles.

Wes Hunter finds a hands-off rest on a large break on Poetry Pink, Rainbow Slabs to prepare for the crux of the route.

Slab/edge resting exercise – Balance on two footholds on a slab. Try facing into the rock and sideways. Which is easier?

Then try placing one or both knees against the rock, does it feel easier to maintain your balance?

Slab and ledge resting tips

Stand sideways on to the rock.

Use one or both knees for stabilisation.

Try to rest/shake out the calf muscle on slabs.

Getting a hands-off rest on a thin slab, (inset) by placing the knees against the wall, you make a stable platform.

CORNER REST

Indoor climbing walls can be monotonously two dimensional, but outside the rock is multi-faceted. One of the biggest challenges to moving your climbing outdoors is the transition into the third dimension. One of the most common features on rock routes is the corner, groove or scoop. These can allow you to take a break in some quite impressive positions.

Put a foot on either wall of the corner and imagine a line connecting your toes, balance by leaning in to place your belly button (a rough guide to your centre of gravity) inside this line. With your centre of gravity outside this line your body will fall outwards, unless you hold on with your hands.

Bridging out allows a rest on some quite impressive terrain.

The belly button rule – if it is inside an imaginary line between your toes you will fall into the rock, and balance.

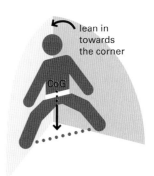

lean in towards the corner

CoG

Corner rest exercise – Bridge out across a corner, groove or scoop.

Move into and away from the corner. Where is the point where you fall backwards and forwards? Consider your belly button.

Let yourself fall forwards. Can you take your hands off and balance on your shoulder? Try turning to face left and then right, so that you can rest on your back or drop your knee (see photos below). Does it feel more or less secure?

Face left, right and into the corner on steeper terrain and on poorer footholds. Does it become easier or harder? Experiment with a variety of foot positions. How does each feel?

Try bridging wider and wider gaps or greater angles.

A variety of bridging from
(A) wide to (B) narrow,
(C) facing out,
(D) back and footing,
and (E) facing outward
under an overhang.

Bridging tips

Imagine a line between your feet. Keep your belly button inside that line.

Try facing sideways.

Flexibility is really helpful for bridging.

ARÊTE REST

Arêtes offer some of the most aesthetic experiences; despite appearing difficult the art of climbing them well stems from the ability to rest.

Face towards the arête, standing on the outside edge of your foot closest the wall, your other foot then heel hooks the arête and by leaning ever so slightly back you can hold yourself in position with your heel hook, leg and stomach holding the tension.

Alternatively face away from the arête. This time your weight is held by the outside edge of one foot on the edge of the arête. Heelhook a foothold on the same side of the arête with your other foot, use your knee as a brace and lean your weight to the side and you will be able to take your hands off.

(A) the body's weight is supported by the lower foot, the other foot is used to heel hook, stopping the climber falling off backwards. The core muscles maintain tension to lay away from the heel hook. (B) the body's weight is supported by the lower foot, this time the knee and heel of the other leg is being used to brace against the wall and the climber leans away from the arête.

Arête resting exercise – On a slabby arête develop the first rest by using a heel hook around the arête.

Hook your foot in different positions on the arête (really high, really low and somewhere in between). Which feels easier to hold?

Lean towards and away from the arête. Where is the least strenuous point when you take your hands off? Where is the strain felt?

Try out the second rest (where the knee braces the arête). Where is the strain taken? Move your upper body towards and away from the arête. Does it make the rest easier or harder to maintain?

Use both sides of the arête and find other arêtes to practise on. Practising in a variety of situations will make it easier to establish the position. These rests can even be used on overhanging arêtes.

Arête tips

Remember face into the arête or away from it, depending on what rest you are trying.

When facing towards the arête, rest with heel hook.

When facing away use the knee brace.

CHIMNEY REST

Probably the most traditional of climbing territory and sadly often overlooked, the chimney is feared by many. It requires the most three dimensional style of climbing, but with spatial awareness you can use many methods to develop a rest in all manner of places.

Place your back on one wall and feet on the other wall. By pushing one against the other you can maintain a sitting position, this is 'back and footing'.

Back and footing is great in corners and other confined positions, not just chimneys.

Dave Rudkin rests before tackling the 5c roof pitch on Free Stone Henge, Castell Helen, Gogarth.

Mark Reeves back and footing up the iconic grove pitch on The Quarryman. Photo courtesy of Oli Barker.

Chimney exercises – Find a chimney (or a narrow corridor or doorway), lean against one side and walk your feet up the other. Experiment with different foot positions and different widths of chimney.

Also experiment with back and footing across corners.

Climbing a narrow (A)
and wide (B) chimney.

Chimney tips

Look for some form of footholds.

Try to wedge yourself in.

Push against both walls.

ONE-FOOTED REST

Another energy saving rest that requires balance. It relies on counterbalancing your legs and body around a single foothold, using your limbs and body as levers. Once you have mastered this and have developed the necessary hip flexion it can allow respite on some pretty steep terrain.

Standing on your toes on a large foothold facing the rock, you may be able to rest your hands, but your calf muscle will become pumped before long. To improve the rest, stand on your heel to rest your calf muscle.

> **One-footed rest exercise** – Face a wall or slab. Stand on your heel on a large hold with the side of your big toe pressing up against the wall. This will put a degree of pressure on your groin. Your other foot can supply support on a hold level or just below the heel.
>
> As you become comfortable, move the other foot lower and lower. More weight will come onto your heel and your other leg will become a counterweight. Keep your weight over the higher foot (keep your belly button over it).

Then see if you can sit on your heel, dangling the other leg as a counterweight.

Progress gradually onto steeper ground, being careful not to go too far too quickly, as the flexion on the hip, knee and groin take a degree of muscular development to avoid injury.

On steeper ground you will need to cam your foot against the rock for greater leverage. Having sat on your heel, imagine that there is a button on the rock right next to your big toe – try and push that button with the side of your big toe.

From standing on the foothold (1) move your foot so that your weight is taken by the heel of the foot (2) then drop the other foot down onto a lower hold in a bicycle position (3) before eventually dropping down so low that you are sat on the heel, and the other leg is just hanging like a counterweight (4).

One-footed rest tips

Develop this slowly, as the full rest puts considerable strain on your hip, knee and groin.

Much of the additional strain is placed on the core muscles of the stomach.

You can help the rest by using the outside edge of the trailing foot to push on a foothold in a kind of bicycle manoeuvre.

Moving Up

Omar Shavit rocking his
way to success on the slate
classic Horse Latitudes,
Rainbow Slab Area.

It's time to combine and develop your techniques – to work your way up between places of rest and conserve as much energy as possible on the way. These exercises look at moving up over a few more typical features of a climb and some of the tactics for conquering them.

ROCK-OVERS

One of the more basic climbing movements (which you will have worked out for yourself no doubt) – how to transfer your weight from one foot to the next. Be aware of your centre of gravity (usually around your belly button). The key is to rock your weight from one foot to the other fairly quickly and hit the next point of balance before moving on.

> **Rock-over exercises** – Standing on the floor, raise your foot onto a bench and bounce up onto this foot. You have just performed a rock-over. This can be done with your hands at first, but eventually you should be able to manage it without by gauging the amount of force needed to just arrive in balance. Too much and you fall over the foot you are rocking onto, too little and you end up back on the foot you started from.

The rock-over, the most simple of climbing movements, but one that can be fine-tuned for maximum efficiency.

Rocking over onto a chair/bench.

Move onto a higher bench or a table. Swap feet and try again.

Try the move on a slabby wall, rocking up onto a foothold without using your hands. Emphasise a dynamic and speedy movement to a point of balance. Visualise the next point of balance as your belly button or head moving to directly over the foot you are about to rock-over onto.

Now link a series of moves from foot to foot, each time concentrating on that point of balance.

Rocking over from standing on the floor, a quick movement to re-establish yourself on a balanced position stood on the next hold, with the climbers belly button directly in line with the foot.

The plumbline helps you visualise when you have reached a point of balance, when the weight is directly over the foot.

You can demonstrate the shift of your centre of gravity from one foot to the other with a water bottle or weight hung from a belt in the small of your back (roughly where your centre of gravity normally is). The plumbline will hang directly over the foot you are balanced on.

Try all this blindfolded (or just close your eyes). You will need to rely on your sense of balance, rather than vision.

Advanced rock-over exercises – With well developed flexibility you can attempt to place your foot beside your hand into a rock-over. This high stepping rock-over is particularly useful for the short, as well as on hard slabs. This will place strain on your groin, so build up slowly.

To achieve a high step you may have to lean back off your hands to get your feet high. You may also have to smear with your lower foot, padding your feet up in order to reach the foothold you want. Try to do this quickly to conserve your arm strength.

A high stepping rock-over, where you match hand and foot before rocking over.

The rock-over and stepping through to the outside edge.

Rock-over tips

Move fluidly, carried by momentum, between one foot and the other.

Hands can help you initiate and stop movement.

Concentrate on coming to rest on one foot in balance.

Stand side on.

Pivot from facing one way to the other as you alternate the direction you are headed.

CORKSCREW ROCK-OVERS & THE RULE OF OPPOSITES

Similar to the rock-over as it essentially involves the transfer of weight from one foot to the other. Its difference comes from pivoting during the movement phase so that you arrive at the next point of balance on your outside edge, which as we have learnt from earlier exercises is more efficient. This keeps your hips and centre of gravity as close to the rock as possible, reducing the leverage onto your hands as you lean back.

A basic corkscrew rockover, with a pivot towards the end of the movement.

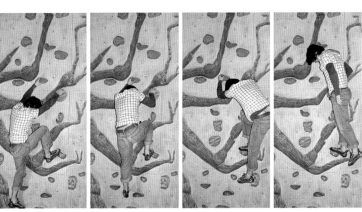

Corkscrew rock-over exercises – Raise your foot onto a hold using the inside edge of your shoe. Use handholds for balance and rock-over. As you reach the point of balance pivot around on your foot to end up on the outside edge of your shoe to finish.

Then try the pivot during the rock-over rather than at the end of the movement. Pivot round on the higher foot as you move up to arrive at the new point of balance on the outside edge of your shoe.

Link a series of movements from foot to foot, concentrating on putting the twist in as you rock-over and arriving at the point of balance on the outside edge of your shoe.

Compare this corkscrew rock-over to a standard rock-over; which feels easier? How do they compare on short distances and at the limit of your stretch? Short step or high step? Which type is easier on slabs, vertical walls or overhangs?

Pick a foothold directly above the lower hold and then a hold way out to the side. Try moving the pivot to before, during and after the rock-over. Does one need a stronger grip with your hands?

The cork screw
rock-over.

The rule of opposites

A standard rock-over tends to make us move left and right as we step up, whereas a corkscrew rock-over or a step through can help us to go directly up. Stepping across the centre line of your body and trying to stay sideways uses opposing left and right limbs.

So the rule is: The upper body uses the opposite limb to the lower body (left hand, right foot – right hand, left foot). Combine this with facing towards the hand you are using at the time.

Using the rule of opposites: Stepping up onto the outside edge of the left rock shoe, and using mainly the right hand to lay away, and left hand to press down.

Rule of opposites exercises – Use only opposite limbs left hand – right foot and vice versa.

Emphasise the direction that you are facing; if you are pulling on your right hand then face to the right.

Now try making the pivot before you rock over so that you are always rocking over onto the outside edge of your foot. This will help keep your centre of gravity closer to the wall, reducing the leverage on your hands.

You may find that if the step is too high you will have to do the twist during the rock-over.

Experiment with higher and higher steps, reaching them using sidepulls.

How does the rule of opposite feel? Easier or harder when stepping through? Is there a height of step when stepping through that it is easier to twist before, during or after the rock-over?

Corkscrew rock-over/rule of opposites tips

Move fluidly, carried by momentum, between one foot and the other.

The pivot can happen before, during or after the movement.
Experiment with what feels better when doing short or long steps, stepping out to the side, into the centre, or across the body.

When you pivot before the movement you will back step onto the hold.

Use opposite limbs.

Face the right direction.

CORNERS

Bridgeable features often provide ways to rest the pulling muscles in our arms and make upward progress.

Corner exercises – Placing both hands on one wall of a corner, walk your feet up the other.

Try this again with only one arm, and then the other. Keep the arm straight, and pivot around the wrist and shoulder, as you walk your feet up the wall.

Put a foot on one wall and using the palms of your hands, palm up the other wall, pivoting around the foot. Now do the same with the other foot. Climb a simple corner, instead of pulling on holds use your palms and feet.

Another trick for ascending corners and grooves is 'back and footing', see Chimney Rest earlier page 96.

Climb a corner with as many hands-off rests as possible, by bridging and back and footing.

Climb again but your hands can only grip as if you were holding a cup of tea.

(A) pivoting around your feet using your palms uses different muscles to pulling down on holds.

(B) pivoting around your palms by walking your feet up the wall.

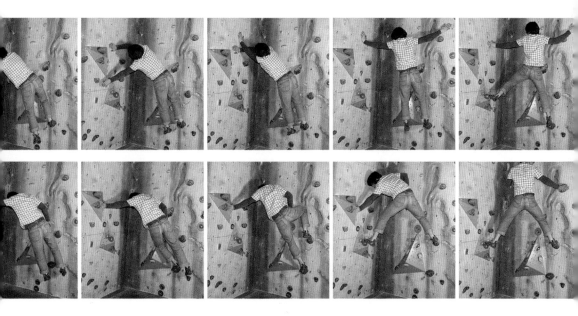

By pushing the left arm against the right leg you can free the left foot and move up and repeat on the opposite side.

Corner tips

Use your hand to pivot around your feet and feet to pivot around hands.

Palming off the wall uses different muscles to pulling down on holds.

Rest whenever you can, both bridging and 'back and footing'.

THE LAYBACK

George Manley laybacks the crack on Merlin Direct, Tremadog, HVS

Cracks, corners or arêtes, many can be conquered by a series of layback moves. Get it right and you can move quickly and efficiently; get it wrong and you'll have a strenuous off-balance nightmare. The basic principle is the rule of opposites, trying to use left hand against right foot and vice versa.

> **Layback exercises** – Step onto a vertical wall with your left hand and left foot directly in line with one another and lean right, laying away from the holds. Now push off the wall with your right hand. What happens?
>
> Step back onto the same holds using the rule of opposites. Face in the direction of the hand (so if using right hand and left foot face right) and lean away from your hand. Push yourself away from the wall with your left hand. What happens this time? Is it more or less stable than the using limbs from the same side of the body?

Using the same side of the body (right hand and right foot) the body makes a natural hinge letting the body swing out like a barn door. Using opposite limbs (right hand, left foot) helps to resist the effect.

To layback efficiently the trick is to know when to transfer the weight from one set of limbs to the next.

Get back onto the wall, using the rule of opposites. With your foot 'accelerate' and 'decelerate' like you would in a car. Is there a point you can 'decelerate' to where you start to feel the 'barn door effect'? Try to hold this position. Then 'accelerate' as hard as you can. Which felt easier to maintain balance?

Try the exercise again. This time the 'accelerator' is a button under your big toe. See whether you can get the same effect just by pressing the button lightly.

Find a corner, arête or flake and link some laybacking movements together, concentrating on keeping your arms straight. Then add the rule of opposites. Does this help you stay in balance? Lead with the same hand, keeping the outside shoulder lower than the inside one.

As you acquire skill and shoulder strength, it will become easier to cross hand over hand.

Try again, this time crossing hand over hand as you layback up the feature. Is this easier or harder than leading with the same hand? Which feels more in balance?

Think about your feet. Layback up a feature three times, on the first go keep your feet really low, the second go bring them really high, and the third go somewhere in between. Which feels easier? Do different rock types make a difference (slate vs grit)?

Laybacking tips

Concentrate on keeping your arms straight, pivoting around the hands and shoulders, using your feet to drive you up.

Between movements try and develop opposite limbs taking the strain.

If it is a short section of laybacking try and climb it as quickly as possible to a rest.

Laybacking a wide crack can be like climbing an arête. You can heel or toe hook the crack too.

THE MANTELSHELF

It's great party game too. With a large and stable table, reverse mantel one end, traverse underneath it and mantel back on top the other side.

A common move, yet one of the hardest to master. In indoor walls and on sports climbs we rarely make the transition from the vertical to the horizontal. A tricky or poorly executed 'mantel' will feel insecure and off balance; done well they can be effortless. A mantelshelf is best described as the 'getting out of the swimming pool move'.

There are four essential movements which make up a mantelshelf; press up, place your foot or heel over the edge, turn your opposite hand toward the foot that you moved up (rotating it palm down), followed by pushing down off your palm and rotating/rolling your shoulder over it. As you pivot the rest of your body will follow.

'...on an old fashioned mantelpiece it is easy to raise yourself on your hands, but surprisingly awkward to obtain a footing; a very delicate balance is needed. It is a good plan to first crowd the mantelpiece with all the ornaments that you most detest – those china dogs presented by Uncle Joe can take a front place. A slight slip on your part – most unfortunate of accidents – and they are no more.'

– Colin Kirkus

(1) Press up. (2) Moving the foot up, the closer to the hands the better. (3) Turn the hand furthest from the foot round to a palm. (4) Roll your shoulder over your hand, and slowly stand up maintain balance as you go.

Mantelshelf exercises – Use a low wall, this should be relatively easy as you can grasp the opposite side of the wall. Place your foot as close to your hand as you can and then as far away as possible. Which makes the move easier? Then try a narrower wall, sturdy fence or gate.

Then onto a small boulder, keeping both hands on the edge (not reaching over to any holds). It may feel as if you might fall off backwards.

Then find a ledge on a vertical wall, or a sturdy mantelpiece. The wall will get in the way, feeling like it is pushing you out. For the most extreme mantelshelf, try the horizontal bar of a soccer goal post.

Mantelshelf tips

Place your foot on a good hold.

Use your palm to push down.

Get your shoulder and belly button over the foot.

On a vertical wall, stepping onto the ledge sideways will help keep your centre of gravity close to the wall.

ARÊTES

Many arêtes will succumb to a series of laybacks. To climb them well requires kinaesthetic awareness of the various positions of rest open to you. The change of angle around an arête can be advantageous, if your feet are on one side laying away from the arête even a small hand hold on the other side can become a jug.

Mark Evans laybacking up the overhanging Pacman Arête, Llanberis Pass.

Climbing an arête.

Arête exercises – Layback up an arête, using the rule of opposites. You may need to move from one side of the arête to the other as hand and footholds dictate. Try moving around the arête from one side to the other.

Recall the hands-off rests from page 95. Climb an arête with as many hands-off rests as possible.

Arête tips

Find as many rests as you can.

Pivot around your hands by driving from the feet.

Practise moving around arêtes from left to right.

Most of the time you will climb facing towards the arête.

CHIMNEYS

Climbing chimneys efficiently is difficult, as much of the time actually moving up requires an energy sapping 'thrutching' that tires the whole body. The only respite you get is when resting in between struggling upward. The best psychological approach for many chimneys is one of rugged determination and that given a good fight you will succeed.

Chimneys cover a vast range of width of cracks; essentially anywhere you can fit a body. Move up by locking or wedging one part of your body which then allows you to move another part. By repeating this wedge-move-wedge-move it is possible to edge your way upwards.

Back and footing
up a chimney

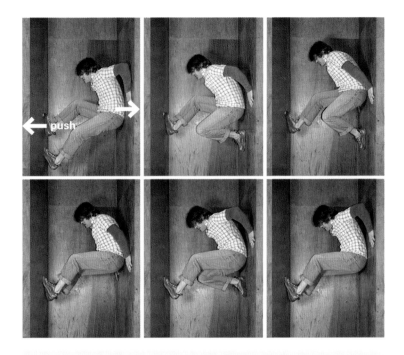

Chimney exercise – Find a chimney, doorway or corner and place your back against one wall and feet against the other and try and sit down in a wedged position.

Push off one foot and your back and move the other foot up and then wedge yourself off the higher foot and your back.

Using your hands against the wall your back is on, thrutch your back upwards and attain another sitting position. By repeating this movement it is possible to edge your way upwards.

Chimney tips

Although it is possible to climb a totally smooth chimney, placing your feet on footholds or edges makes the whole process a lot easier.

You will have a fight on your hands.

You can often rest by simply sitting down, it is the thrutching upwards that is exhausting.

Decide which way round you are going to face before you start. Try the first move facing one way and then reverse down and try it the other, decide which is easier before committing yourself. It will often be impossible to turn around half-way up.

Thin chimneys are harder to climb, unforgiving on the body, totally claustrophobic and requiring a lot of energy to move up. Improvisation is the answer, but the principle is the same, wedge-shuffle-shuffle-wedge. It will often be impossible to see your feet, or arms for that matter; so take note of prominent foot holds as they pass your face and struggle relentlessly until you can feel your feet on them (perhaps your only chance of a rest).

Struggling up a constricted chimney.

ROOFS

Moving around roofs can be strenuous on the arms, the trick is to move past the obstacle as quickly as possible to a rest above.

Place gear close up under the roof and even above the lip of the roof if you can reach. Going up and down a few times may give you a clear picture of where hand and footholds are. Having placed gear or taken a peek over the lip descend to a rest below the roof to prepare yourself. When you decide to go, do so with determination and don't stop until you're above the roof where it will be far less strenuous to stop and place gear.

Roof exercises – Below the roof find a good rest and look at the moves above. When you have an idea of how to proceed, move up until you are faced with the need to step your feet over the roof.

With strength you will be able to step your foot over the lip of the roof, but to start with and on harder routes you will find it easier to place your knee over the roof to rock-over and step up with your other foot. Don't stop until you are stood above the roof.

(A) Sequence of movements using first the knee to move over a roof, and then (B) without the aid of the knee.

Dave Rudkin makes a 'bomb-shelter' or cluster of runners before a difficult section to boost his confidence before he tackles the roof of Free Stonehenge, E7 6b.

Roof tips

Standing sideways before, after and as you climb through the roof will save energy. You may even find a hands-off rest.

Move as swiftly as possible through the roof.

Rest after you have stepped over the roof.

OVERHANGING WALLS

By its very nature an overhanging wall is going to be strenuous. At lower grades the chances are that any steep rock will be reasonably short lived and you will be able to rest at either the top or bottom of the section.

Just like a roof find a good rest below a steep section and place gear as high as possible. Whilst stood below try and work out the sequence of moves for your hands and feet. You may be able to mark footholds with a dab of chalk to help you spot them when you are committed to the hard climbing.

After assessing the moves you face a decision. If the section is short, commit to climbing quickly and confidently through it. If on the other hand you are unsure then you can climb up a few moves and place some higher gear before reversing back to the rest. By repeatedly going up and down you can place progressively higher runners and also start to work out the complete sequence to overcome the obstacle. If you choose to yo-yo up and down like this, keep in mind whether the moves you are making are reversible and just how long can you hang on in that position before you fail? You'll need to balance working out the sequence versus the need to blast on through the crux before you become too pumped.

Arms straight and driving from the feet, minimise the strain on your arms. Climber; Mike Hamel at Craig Y Forwen.

Overhanging walls exercise – From a good rest below a steep section, work out your probable sequence of moves and where possible, mark any useful footholds as far as you can reach with chalk. Then give it a go. If you find extra holds that would make the sequence easier, reverse back down to the rest and try again. Repeat this until you are ready to move through the whole section. Then take a few deep breaths and tackle the section with determination.

To keep your arms straight, imagine there is an iron bar down them, or get some large cardboard tubes that will keep them straight!

There are some more techniques covered in the next section, Advanced Technique & Bouldering (see p117).

Overhang tips

The principles of climbing sideways and using opposite limbs are key.

By getting your feet high and keeping your arms straight you can drive yourself upwards with your legs.

Moving swiftly through a steep section of rock is going to use far less energy than hanging around on every hold.

Sometimes it is possible to reduce the angle at which you are climbing by finding grooves and corners to bridge out on.

Nick Bullock attacks the final steep wall on the awesome Right Wall (E5), Dinas Cromlech.

Advanced Technique & Bouldering

Unknown Climber on Cross Fader, Cromlech Boulders. Bouldering is a key ingredient for getting physically stronger and technically better.

Bouldering to push your climbing standard is not as new a pastime as people would have you believe. Oscar Eckenstein talked about bouldering technique classes back in 1901 and many climbers used roadside boulders to hone their skill from the 1960s onwards. Today it is has become a genre of climbing which some people pursue exclusively. Guidebooks have been written and grading systems developed; the John 'Vermin' Sherman V grade, Fontainebleau grade, British technical grade and the gritstone B grade.

Bouldering has become popular as a form of training and in the pursuit of fun. The techniques for bouldering and harder rock climbing take a great deal more strength, which distinguishes them from techniques common to the easy and mid-grade routes that most people start out climbing on.

Bouldering introduces us to new ways of climbing through experimentation and observing other climbers on the same problems. The social nature of bouldering, with people taking turns at the same problem, is like an im-promptu movement workshop.

Bouldering allows us to dabble in moves way harder than you are likely to find on a route that you wish to lead. It gives us a wider understanding of how to get the best out of hand and foot holds through body position, as well as developing strength and technique in relative safety, close to the ground. It allows greater repetition of the moves too, which will help to reinforce techniques in your subconscious and gives a greater variety of movements when you come to tackle difficulties on a route. Well worth considering given that it takes around 100 repetitions of a movement to lay down that movement memory. Bouldering will develop specific arm, finger and upper body strength, as well as help to develop your core strength, which are all a key to climbing steeper and harder routes.

Hand and footholds

Many hand and footholds on routes and boulder problems require a degree of fine tuning when it comes to finding the best part to hold and the best body position to adopt. It often boils down to your own style which is affected by your body type, sex and height. A body position that works for one person won't necessarily work for another. Finding what works for you is a matter of experimentation.

Get a friend to select the holds to use before stepping onto the wall or play hold twister. Photo: Paul Smith from *Climbing Games* (Pesda Press).

Hand and foot hold exercise – Find a boulder with a large selection of holds, simply choose any four hand and footholds and just step off the ground. Move your feet and turn your body to find the easiest position to hang those holds.

Repeat this on a variety of holds; slopers, sidepulls, undercuts, crimps and jams. Try different hand positions and hold orientations or get friends to pick out holds for you.

Then looking at the holds before you step on try to figure out the best position. Get into that position, before trying others. Was it the best position?

Then link the holds you are on with another. While one position will be easier to hold, you will more than likely have to change your position to reach another hold. Once you reach the new hold bring your body back into a resting position. Complete a few set boulder problems with this rest – reach – rest approach.

This exercise will hopefully help illustrate the difference between hanging on holds and making upwards movement.

On an indoor wall you can play a game of hold twister, to encourage you to attempt positions that you might not have thought possible. Holding extreme positions is highly useful when bouldering.

Heel and toe hooking

Very useful in taking the weight off your arms on many arêtes, overhangs or roofs. On steeper ground a heel or toe hook can make the difference between hanging a hold and falling off, as you start using your feet as pulling limbs rather than points to push off or pivot around.

Heel and toe hooks are key to this Parisellas classic Lou Ferrino (V10). Matt Clifford sets up for another power move up the hanging rib.

Heel and toe hooking exercise – An easy and fun way to try this out is the table traverse. Find a sizeable and sturdy table (you might require some friends to sit on and stabilise it so that it doesn't topple over). From sitting underneath the table, traverse it's length by using your feet as you would your hands, 'grasping' the edge of the table by hooking your toe or heel over it. You can start on top of the table, traverse under it's length and mantel back on top the other side.

Another more practical application is to use the heel as a pulling limb on a overhanging arête. Use your feet to toe and heel hook your way up as you climb. Try to maintain contact at all times and do not cut loose.

Examples of hooking the heel around an arête (pulling on it helps ease the strain on the arms).

Drop knee

The drop knee (or Egyptian) forces one foot to pivot and the knee to bend to bring that shoulder and hip closer to the rock, taking weight off the hand on the same side in preparation to move. It helps to lock your body into a better position and makes it easier to hang the holds. It's most useful on steep walls but it can be used to great effect in a variety of climbing situations as it helps put the body side on to the rock, moving the centre of gravity close to the wall.

(A) From facing straight on. (B) Moving into a drop knee position like this takes weight off the left hand and (C) brings your body closer to the wall.

Rotate your leg so it is side onto the wall and try and push the knee towards the other foot, bracing against the other foothold out to the side, in a way 'back and footing' the two holds. This will bring your hip into contact with the wall, increasing your reach.

Drop knee exercise – On a moderately overhanging wall, find a position facing the wall on four holds. Reach up as far as you can with one hand, and note how far you can reach and how strenuous it was on your hands.

Then reach up with the same hand using the same holds, but before you reach, turn away from that hand, drop your knee on that side and get your hip to touch the wall. Really push against either foot and reach up. Was it easier on your hands? Could you reach any further?

Try experimenting with different footholds and using sidepulls. How far can you reach?

Knee-bars and foot-locks

On very steep terrain, knee-bars and foot-locks help to take the weight off the arms and at times they can allow hands-off rests in impressive situations. In bouldering the technique is common even on moderate problems.

Similar to jamming, use your lower limbs to brace and lever (using core strength), transferring the weight from your hands to your legs. Cracks aren't necessary, instead look for advantageous footholds, changes of angle and flakes.

They are most useful when the body is horizontal so require good core strength and flexibility. Unless you can lift your foot to your hand you may not be able to find position in which these techniques are beneficial.

> **Knee-bar exercise** – Finding a good place to use a knee-bar is an art in itself. It's something of a misnomer as it is the thigh that you brace against. You need a hold to place your foot on and a wall, roof or large sidepull to brace your thigh against. Look for a gap that is shorter than your lower leg. Your thigh takes the pressure as you lean away from the brace.

(A) Knee-bar in the corner. (B) Using a foot-lock to reach far to one side of the footholds.

> **Foot-lock exercise** – Use your heel and toe to cam against each other, allowing you to pull on your foot with your leg and core. You will need to be nearly horizontal for this to aid you. See the example foot-lock and find some places to use them. Beware that if you fall it is possible to leave your foot behind, resulting in twisted ankles or knees and more than likely face planting the ground.

Kinaesthetic awareness

This is bodily awareness – knowing what each limb is doing, where it is and the consequence to your balance when it moves. We use points of contact with the wall like a series of hinges about which our centre of gravity pivots.

On easier climbing this is slow and controlled but as the climbing becomes more difficult the movements become quicker, momentum and precision is needed. Learn to predict the consequences of a move and you will be able to adapt it to minimise the unwanted side effects.

Concentrate on fluid and dynamic movements and try to predict what re-moving one limb might do to the stability of your position. Experiment with different styles of movement like swinging monkey-like between holds.

> **Kinaesthetic exercise** – On a traverse make a step or reach just be-yond your reach by pivoting on your foot and dropping onto the hold. Try this in both directions. What happens when you catch the hold? Can you tense parts of your body to reduce the 'barn door' effect?

Reaching beyond your range. Can you control the 'barn door' effect as you grasp the final hold?

> Traverse again making some over-exaggerated cross-throughs, and then let your body unwind. Try and predict the swing, and to a certain extent let your body go with it. Repeat the exercise and experiment using body tension and the direction your body is facing to reduce the swing.

Exaggerated cross-throughs. Can you use the swing to your advantage, or reduce it?

One handed traverse
on a vertical wall.

On a vertical wall or steep slab try making a series of moves with only one hand. Predict how your balance will change once you have arrived at the new position. Experiment with different foot positions, or flagging one foot as a counterweight to maintain a stable position after the move.

Experiment with moving both hands simultaneously to holds close by. How does this affect your balance?

Dynamic moves

Whether a hold is just slightly out of reach and requires a little lunge or the holds are a long way away and require a jump to reach, these movements require kinaesthetic awareness of your body's movement and proprioception of the end point or 'deadpoint'. Like most movements they have a beginning, a middle and an end – the set up, the jump and the catch.

'Static' vs 'dynamic' movement

In climbing a 'static' movement is one that is made slowly and in control. A 'dynamic' move requires speed, accuracy and momentum to reach a hold.

Deadpoint

Imagine leaping up for a hold in slow motion, your body moves upwards and at the top of the upward movement you are momentarily motionless, before gravity makes you drop. This instant of weightlessness is the 'deadpoint'. It takes practice to time and judge a jump or lunge so that the apex or deadpoint of the jump coincides with grasping the hold you are reaching for.

Contact finger strength

When making dynamic moves, the ability to grasp a hold quickly is key. The speed at which we can latch onto a hold is often referred to as 'contact finger strength' – our ability to engage as many muscle fibres as possible in as short a time as possible. When we are fatigued it is often this contact finger strength that we lose first, which can lead to injury as your technique becomes sloppy.

Lunging

This requires power and control. The aim is to use enough power to reach the hold, but not too much, as you don't want to overshoot the target.

Lunging exercise – Lunges require a great deal of contact finger strength. This is the ability to rapidly latch a hold as soon as you reach it. Jump off the ground to a hold, and try to latch it as quickly as possible as soon as you feel it under your hands. Use a large hold first before moving onto smaller holds, as the exercise puts a lot of strain on your fingers. Concentrate on reaching a hold at the apex of your upward movement, 'the dead point', where you feel momentarily weightless.

Next find a hold that you can just reach in a slow and static way. Then practise reaching for it dynamically, driving with your feet and pulling rapidly with your arms. To begin with don't grab the hold you are lunging for, instead just tap it. Concentrate on the tap coming at the dead point. Once you are happy that you are tapping the hold at the dead point, try catching the hold. Start with a large positive hold. Expect your body to completely cut loose when you reach the hold and predict just where it is likely to swing. Can you reduce the swing? Can you do anything to help stop your feet cutting loose? Try this exercise – with both left and right hands.

Lunging for a hold. The climber has to use body tension to keep his feet on the footholds.

Campus exercise – On the large rungs of a campus board try a slow pull up. If you can do this, try doing one as quickly and explosively as you can. With practice and as you develop power you will be able to move off the rung you are on. At first don't try and hang another rung, just see how far up the campus board you can tap with both hands, or momentarily leave the rung you are on before grabbing it again. This exercise requires a lot of finger strength, and can easily result in injury, so use big holds at first and build up slowly.

Campus board exercises: (A) Leading with one hand but only touching the rung you are aiming for, then instantly dropping back to the starting position. (B) Going with both hands simultaneously, here rungs 1 to 3.

Dynos

A true 'dyno' is when all parts of the body are momentarily out of contact with the rock, a kind of 'slam dunk' onto a hold. Done well it's bold and impressive, a popular way of showboating. The movement breaks down again to setting up, jumping and catching.

Dyno exercise – Get used to your body pivoting around your feet. Pull onto the wall, using big holds for hands and feet in a frog-like position. Hang on your arms as far out on the holds as you can and then pull yourself in quickly. Your body will pivot around your feet. Let yourself drop back on the holds to hanging as far out as possible. Feel how your body is momentarily weightless as you pull in. As you gain confidence, momentarily let go of the holds, before dropping back onto them. Then try a hand clap at the moment of weightless, before dropping back onto the holds. When you have reached this stage you are ready to progress to the launching or jumping phase.

Working on the set-up for the dyno. Swinging out and in, and letting go at the deadpoint of the movement.

At the moment you would let go and clap your hands, drive up with both feet and try and touch the wall as high up as possible with both hands. Don't try to catch the holds, just tap the wall and push yourself off backwards. Eventually you will be able to accurately judge the distance to two holds (preferably large ones).

Swinging in and launching up the wall as far as possible.

Swinging in and launching up the wall and then catching the holds.

When you are tapping the holds consistently at the dead point of your upward movement, commit to grabbing the holds with both hands simultaneously. Eventually you will be able to reach holds that are so far away your feet will leave their footholds. Progress gradually to this stage by either lower starting holds or higher finishing holds, keeping your feet on the footholds.

It's a common mistake to lead with one hand and following with the other, the trick is to be confident and commit to going with both hands at the same time. If you have this problem go back to start of the progression and concentrate on going with both hands simultaneously.

Redpointing

We owe the word 'redpoint' to Kurt Albert who developed many new routes in the 1970s at Frankenjura, Bavaria. He would put a red cross on fixed equipment that he had successfully eliminated as points to rest on. Eventually when the route was climbed in its entirety without using any form of aid from the fixed equipment he would paint a red spot at the bottom of the route, a Rotpunkt or 'point of red', to signify that the route had been climbed entirely free.

These ascents were achieved through a great deal of practice. Practising the route so well that they barely had to think about any move, to climb way beyond their normal ability. Like a dancer learning a new routine, at first they will make plenty of mistakes, but with time and practice they will successfully link the whole routine together seamlessly and it will appear almost effortless.

This practice is now used by traditional climbers to climb the hardest of routes in the E7 and above grades. By practising the route over and over the climber has the knowledge that they can do the route on top rope and would have succeeded numerous times before leading a dangerous route. This type of ascent is referred to as headpointing.

The process comes down to a systematic breaking down of routes and boulder problems into set sequences of hand, foot and body movements. The more you repeat the move the more you start to rely on muscle memory, where you are essentially remembering how hard and fast to pull on different holds to reach the next, and what to do with your feet when you have reached the next holds. By practising the route over and over you train specifically for the route, and learn to make the right moves almost instinctively. More than this you have shown your brain that you can do the moves, meaning that you also have the psychological edge.

This mental advantage is key to redpoint success, as often the mere thought of failure is enough to bring just that. Barriers like this are hard to overcome and, in bouldering, can lead to great frustration when you fail repeatedly on the same move time and time again.

Redpointing boulder problems means we are at the upper limit of our ability. This requires total concentration and commitment.

Redpointing exercise – In order to learn how to redpoint you need to find something too hard for you to climb first time, like a boulder problem you can do most of the moves on but not link. Break the route down into bits you can climb and bits you can't and first work on the moves you can't. Pull onto the route or problem by the specific move you can't do, and practise it over and over. This can take weeks, months or years until eventually you will do that move. As you start to make individual moves try and link more and more moves until you can link overlapping sections.

The next step is climbing the problem from the start to just after the crux and from just before the crux to the end. From here it is a just a matter of trying to redpoint the route or boulder problem linking the overlapping sections.

Redpoint mentality

See Mind Games (p159) for visualisation and imagery techniques.

There are a couple of tricks that will help you succeed. The first is rest, if you have just been practising the moves you need to allow enough time for your muscles to recover. You should also warm up well to delay the onset of becoming pumped.

Stand below the line and visualise yourself doing the moves; you have practised them so much you will probably be able to mimic the movements on the ground, including when you breathe, when you are relaxed and when you are pulling as hard as possible. Warm up your mind for the moves ahead of you. It reinforces your memory of the sequence and focuses you on positive thinking.

The final step before you climb is physical preparation. Brush and chalk the holds, clean your boots and dry them until they squeak, to give you that extra edge when it comes to sticking to the footholds. Find a positive frame of mind, 'I can link this', 'I am going to succeed'. Follow your ritual, a few deep breathes, adjust your hands and feet on the starting holds and with conviction pull on them and give it more gusto than you ever have before.

Climbing the final steep crack of Left Wall, Llanberis Pass.

Putting It All Together

Someone putting it all
together at the Upper
Tier Tremadog.

Hopefully by now you will have developed some energy saving habits, as well as an understanding of how to carry on learning. After all it will be your own discoveries at the crag that will carry you above and beyond.

Even a single pitch might require all of the skills outlined so far. The trick is to identify the different styles you will need to use – you need to be able to 'read' the route. To be adept at reading a route the skills and movements of climbing will already be subconscious. Your body needs to have used the movements hundreds of times before it starts to lay down subconscious muscle memory.

Visualising the route
helps switch your brain
to climbing mode.

There are a couple of ways you can help: Think about climbing whenever you can! By thinking of the movement you are exercising some of the same brain functions you use when you are actually climbing. By climbing as quickly as possible, quicker than you can think through the moves, you exercise your subconscious skills.

Subconscious climbing exercise – Find a pitch that you should find relatively easy to climb and climb it as quickly as possible. The guide for how quickly should be the point at which you feel that you are making moves before you have had the time to really think about what you are doing. You may be using bad technique, so climb the same pitch slowly. Did one feel less efficient? Repeat this exercise to see if you start to become more efficient at speed. Use familiar and unfamiliar routes.

GUIDEBOOKS

The ability to read routes is pointless if you can't find the crag. Get yourself some guidebooks; some are pictorial, others are more descriptive; all help you find the crag, the start of the route and the climbing line.

A more traditional hand drawn topo by the Climbers' Club and a modern photo-topo guidebook.

Read the route description carefully and examine the topos. Try to identify key features and landmarks described in the book and visualise the line of the route on the crag. On a multi-pitch route this becomes difficult as part of the crag may be obscured from view. It may be necessary to check the guidebook on the approach to the cliff as you often get a better view of the route.

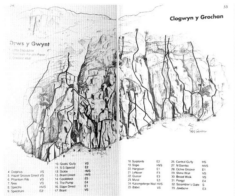

Comparing what you see in the guidebook and on the approach to some crags reveals the whole picture, not possible if you leave it till you are standing at the bottom of the crag.

When people first start using guidebooks they often misinterpret the information, a slight groove becomes a corner, a crack becomes a chimney, etc. The trick is to learn from you mistakes (typically trying to make the description of your chosen route fit the section of cliff you are standing below!)

Guidebook exercise – Before heading to a crag spend some time in the comfort of your own home doing a bit of armchair research. This will help you develop a memory for descriptions and route diagrams, as well as get you fired up to visit new places.

As you approach the crag have the guidebook to hand. If you get a good view of the crag you can identify possible approaches to the bottom of the crag and work out the rough line of one or more of the routes on the crag. This will help you to arrive at the bottom of the route that you wish to climb.

At the bottom of the route read the description again and look at the topo. Your route may not be shown, but the lines of the routes to either side might. Visualise the line of the climb. It can be helpful to ask other climbers around what routes they are climbing but they may be just as lost as you!

If you are setting up a top rope you need to identify features at the top of the crag that will help you find the top of the route. Or alternatively place some rucksacks or a climbing partner just out from the base as a reference point to locate the appropriate place to rig your ropes.

When climbing the route let the belayer have the guidebook and keep it open on the right page, and if you get confused get them to direct you, as they often have a better view of the bigger picture.

Once you have finished the route, try re-writing the description in your own words. Does the guidebook use different words to describe the features and different phrases to describe the climbing?

A guidebook holder is ideal for multi-pitch climbing so you can carry the guidebook up the crag with you and also mark the page.

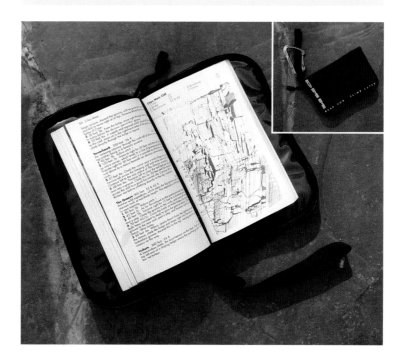

READING ROUTES

Talk to other climbers; they might be able to tell you where they found the going tough or where they found a crucial gear placement. They may also be able draw comparisons with other routes that you have climbed.

As you approach the route and can see the whole thing, note any features that may help you to find your way to the top. Look for obvious rests or gear placements. Binoculars may be useful to examine the route. You may get a better view by climbing an easier adjacent route or on a single pitch climb it may be possible to walk round to the top. The more angles you view the climb from the better the three dimensional image of the route you will have.

Identifying the type of terrain and how best to climb is at the heart of reading a route. Break your route down into sections, ideally between obvious rests. Think about what skills you are likely to need and visualise yourself climbing the moves. As you do this at the base of the route you are switching your brain to climbing mode. You need to continue to read the route as you climb, not only to follow the line but also to react to the terrain and climb using appropriate technique.

Reading routes exercise – Look up at a route from the ground and try to identify the skills you may need, where the rests are, where the crux moves are, what kind of belay awaits at the top of the pitch, etc. Now climb the route and see if it meets your expectations. Take a photocopy of the topo and mark down your thoughts or write them on a piece of notepaper before you climb, so you can review them afterwards. Were you drastically wrong? If so where and why? How could you improve your eye for judging routes?

Try this on every route you climb – you don't always have to take notes. The more your route reading develops the closer to getting things 100% right you will become – although it is unlikely you will ever be totally right!

Reading routes tips

Visualisation is key; you might imagine seeing a line on the rock, hearing yourself talk through the route or recall a written set of instructions.

Your plan may be wrong, the skill of reading a route while climbing is just as important.

Use rests on the route to look at the next section, reformulate your plan and identify the next rest.

Colour coding your route

How you colour in a route will be a personal thing, green climbing for most will be very easy, usually with a good spattering of ledges to rest on.

Orange would be for the blank sections where the holds are smaller, and the rests are further apart. Most of the moves will require a degree of thinking but the rests, climbing and angle of the route will mean that you shouldn't feel like you are getting pumped.

Red is the steep and harder section, maybe just a single move, roof or bulge in the rock. It will be to hard too hang about on these sections and they will require a sense of urgency or power to overcome. Identify a place to rest and/or place gear after them, so that you have a point to aim for.

Visualisation exercise – Draw your route on paper using a colour scheme to indicate different climbing styles; green circle = rest, green = easy, orange = requires a little thought but is not that pumpy, red = hard climbing requiring power, speed and technique (the hardest moves you are capable of and you will become pumped).

Try to visualise your colour coded route on the rock and use this plan to climb the route.

Were there any differences between the plan and the execution? If so did you spot the problem before, during or after you had to climb that section of the route and could you have spotted the problem earlier?

A photo of a colour coded route and written description.

CLIMB UP ONTO THE FIRST LEDGE ARRANGE GEAR AND LOOK AT THE INITIAL CRUX WALL.
LOOK FOR ANY OTHER GEAR BEFORE CRUX THEN MOVE UP PLACE IT AND REVERSE BACK DOWN TO LEDGE.
REST AND COMMIT TO CLIMBING CRUX WHICH FINISHES AT A GOOD JUG AND WIRE.
CONTINUE UP THE PUMPY AND WELL PROTECTED CRACK. THERE IS A POSSIBLE REST ON THE RIGHT WHERE A HVS JOINS THE ROUTE.
MORE PUMPY CLIMBING LEADS TO THE FIRST OF SEVERAL LEDGES AND AN EASING IN THE CLIMBING

Visualisation tips

Some people might find this visualisation technique more useful than a written description.

Try and see your body making the moves. You may see yourself from a third person viewpoint (like a movie) or through your own eyes from a first person viewpoint. Try to feel the moves as well.

By thinking of the moves you are engaging your pre-motor cortex, and turning your mind to climbing mode.

Reading routes tips

Real hands-on experience of using guidebooks and looking at climbs is required to develop this skill. Learn from your mistakes!

STYLE OF ASCENT

To the vast majority of climbers style is less significant than having fun – it is often the more experienced climbers for whom style of ascent becomes important. Regardless of grade or ability, what is important is that you are honest with yourself and others about your ascent. Each style of ascent employs a different set of tactics.

On-sight – climbing up from the ground, and reaching the top of the route without falling off or resting (with little or no prior knowledge of the route).

Flash – similar to the on-sight but you have some prior knowledge of the route, often a description ('beta') of the hard moves or vital gear from someone who has climbed the route. Some even believe that if you know the grade of the route your ascent will not be an on-sight but a flash instead.

Ground up – climbing up from the ground, but you fall off or rest. At this point you don't practise the move but return to the ground and pull the ropes for another attempt. Basically you eventually succeed in climbing the route from the ground up in one effort.

Yo-yo – similar to ground up, however you don't pull the ropes when you lower to the ground, thereby leaving a top-rope to your previous high point.

Dogged/French free – Like the yo-yo ascent but you don't bother to lower to the ground, hanging in your harness to rest. Often used as a method to prepare a route for a redpoint ascent, cleaning holds and practising the hard moves.

Redpoint/headpoint – You will have practised the route extensively. You succeed at the redpoint when you finally make it from the ground to the top of the pitch without falling or resting. 'Redpoint' is more often used to describe hard sport climbing ascent and 'headpoint' for bold traditional routes (practised on a top-rope).

Pete Robins dogging Wild Understatement (F8b) on the way to his redpoint ascent.

Style and tactics

Most climbers go for some form of on-sight or flashed ascent. To succeed you need to have warmed up prior to your attempt; if you do this on a nearby route you may well have a different view of the route you want to climb. Similarly you will get a feel for the crag (general angle of holds, gear, style of climbing, etc.)

It is important to remember that when going for the onsight or flashed ascent you don't have to only climb upwards. There is often an advantage to reversing either to the ground or a ledge or rest. What is important is that if you do down climb you don't weight the rope. By climbing up and down from positions of rest, you will be able to slowly piece together the right sequence of moves on crux sections until it is possible or necessary for you to commit to the crux or difficult section of climbing.

If you fall you will have blown the on-sight, but you can rest on the rope for a moment and contemplate the move you failed, then lower off to climb the route ground up. Having lowered off and pulled the ropes down you need to rest and recover, whilst trying to remember as much about the climbing as you can. With this advantage, on the next attempt you need to save as much energy as possible for the crux, by moving more efficiently and quickly to your previous high point. While you rest imagine yourself back on the route and recall the sequence of moves.

If the route is definitely going to be too hard for you to on-sight or flash then you probably need to employ totally different tactics. You could practise the route on a top rope if it is a traditional route (headpoint) or on lead if it is a sport route (redpoint). Headpointing requires you to top rope the route until you are totally convinced that you can lead climb the route without falling off. This might take a few attempts or years; the point at which you commit to the lead is a very difficult thing to quantify.

With a redpoint, your first attempt is going to be clipping each bolt and resting, looking at the next few moves to the next bolt and resting. You might even employ a clipstick to reach the next bolt. When you have reached the lower off, you will have an idea of where the crux is, and maybe what sections you can link together. On subsequent practises try to link longer sections or work the crux sequence. This is often best done on the lead, as hard redpoints are often so overhanging that you simply can't top rope them. When you are confident that you can link up the route you should commit every move to memory. Until you can visualise every move the chances are that you haven't got the route sufficiently dialled to be successful.

Lead Climbing Techniques

Composed, organised and relaxed. All key attributes of a skilful lead climber. Climber; Omar Shavit on Super Direct, Dinas Mot, Llanberis Pass.

For many people, leading a route is the essence of climbing. There are no shortcuts to mastering the techniques and head games of lead climbing. Learning to lead is about staying as safe as possible by route selection and getting some coaching on placing gear; the rest of the game is confidence, efficiency, tactics and judgement. Tactics were covered in the previous chapter and self confidence is looked at in the next. To fill in some of the gaps, we'll cover here using your rack efficiently and placing gear efficiently.

Consider an inefficient leader. They take wires off one gear loop on their harness and clip them back on another; after a while it can take a minute or two for them to find the size of wire they are looking for. They have chosen to place gear mid-move or from a poor hold; if they made another half move they would be stood in balance and more able to clip easily. Having placed their wire it takes a few attempts for them to clip the rope into the quickdraw. Throughout they are understandably showing signs of stress. Stress makes them a defensive climber rather than a relaxed, lazy and efficient climber.

CLIPPING QUICKDRAWS

There are several correct ways to clip a karabiner as a running belay and many more incorrect ways. You may be surprised how many people get it wrong or fumble every time they go to clip a rope into what can only be described as the most common piece of climbing equipment.

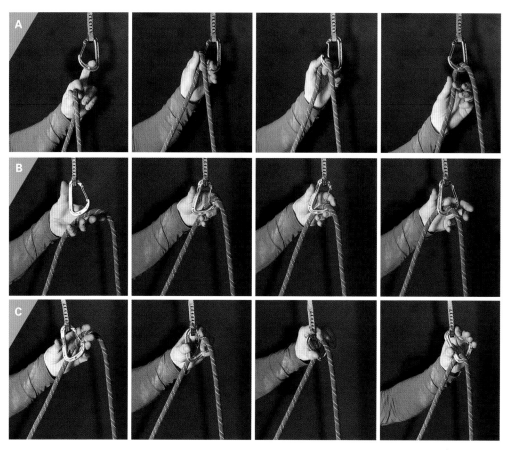

The correct ways to clip quickdraws. (A) Using the middle finger to stabilise the karabiner, and thumb and forefinger to push the rope in. (B) Pinch the karabiner and use the thumb to pinch the rope in. (C) An alternative grip for the thumb pinch. Note that the karabiner is moved to help push the rope into it.

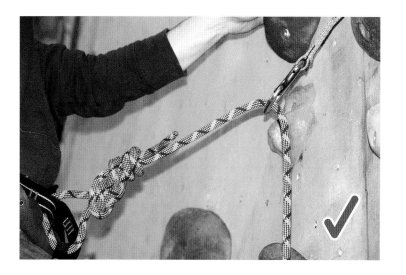

The rope runs up the wall and out through the karabiner towards the climber. This is the correct way to clip a quickdraw.

WARNING – Don't back clip! Back clipping is potentially very dangerous, as the rope can unclip during a fall. Always arrange the quickdraw so there are no twists, then have the rope going into the karabiner from behind and out through the front towards you. If the route is a traverse, consider having the rope running out across the back bar of the karabiner, so the gate is facing the opposite way to the direction of travel. This helps to ensure that in the event of a fall the rope won't potentially unclip as it is pulled across the gate.

Back clipping.

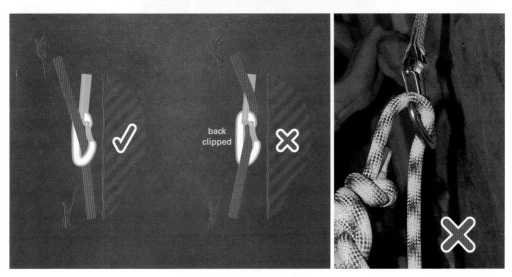

back clipped

On traverses try to ensure the rope comes out and over the back bar (A). The rope runs over the gate in (B), which although not 'back clipped' is still more risky than (A).

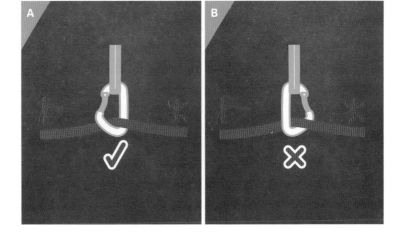

If it is an essential runner consider having two quickdraws in opposition or use a screwgate on the rope instead. This is only really necessary on very run-out routes so that there is absolutely no doubt in your mind that the runner cannot become unclipped from the rope.

If it is vital that a bolt, peg or wire doesn't unclip, consider using (A) quickdraws in opposition or (B) a screwgate.

Clipping quickdraws exercise – While standing on the ground and tied into a rope try clipping a quickdraw within easy reach with your left or right hand, with the gate facing left or right. Then try clipping across your body. Be careful not to 'back clip'.

Turn the karabiner upside down and try again. Which is easier? Hopefully, you will realise that the upside down karabiner is much harder to clip and in future you will take the time to ensure the karabiner is the right way up.

Turn your quickdraw the right way up with the gate facing toward the hand you are going to clip with. Use your middle finger to hook the bottom of the karabiner and your thumb to push the rope in. Practise with both hands.

Next try clipping the quickdraw with the gate facing away from the hand you are about to clip with. This time place your thumb on the back bar of the karabiner and use your index finger to push the rope into the karabiner. Practise with both hands.

Try the same two methods (index finger or thumb stabilising the karabiner) but this time clip across your body.

Repeat practising clipping your quickdraws until you are flawless, remember to add some random variety to your practice.

Try the same clipping exercises standing just off the ground on a slab from a position of balance. The exercise will feel harder because you are concentrating on staying balanced.

Try clipping a quickdraw as high above your head as you can reach, by your head, by your shoulders, by your waist, below your waist and by your feet. Which positions feel easier?

Then try your clipping exercises on a vertical wall and then on an overhanging wall. How much harder is it? Did you use your teeth to help get enough rope in your hand?

WARNING – Using your mouth to help gather the rope up has lead to some nasty injuries, from losing teeth to breaking the lower and in the worst case breaking the upper jaw. Climbers do this all the time, just be aware of the consequences if you fall at that moment.

Clipping traverse race – With a short section of rope set up a few quickdraws on a low level traverse, and have a race. Is it easier to clip when the runners are in front or behind you on the traverse, and does this change depending on what direction you traverse? Try this over a number of weeks, does your time improve? This traversing exercise is good practice for belaying a lead climber too.

ORGANISING YOUR RACK

Choose how to rack your gear, gate in or out, not both ways like this – how will you know to grasp the karabiner without looking?

Using your rack efficiently is also down to dexterity, remaining calm and staying organised. Know what you are carrying where and make sure that when you take something from your rack you return it to the same place. The consequence of a messy rack is wasted time and energy spent looking for the small wires or large Hexs.

The first decision you have to make is gates in or gates out, either all the gates of the karabiners on your gear loops facing in to your body or away. There is no right or wrong way, just one way or the other, not both.

The next problem is what to rack where and, for that matter, what to take with you? Again there is no right answer, but there are a few wrong ones. Your personal preference will quickly fall into place but experimenting with new ideas is helpful, especially on those rainy days when you're stuck at home itching to get out.

WHAT'S IN YOUR RACK?

Karabiners

Wire gates or alloy gates? When it comes to buying snap gate karabiners, the answer really comes down to cost, weight and purpose. A wire gate will save you weight and the gate is less likely to chatter (rapid opening and closing of the gate due to vibrations in the karabiner during a fall), but they are more likely to be opened by catching on the smallest of holds, something that is hard to do with the large diameter of an alloy gate. Older style alloy gate karabiners are easier to rack wires onto because of the wider gate opening. Curved alloy gate karabiners have the advantage of helping guide the rope to clip into the karabiner. On top of this there are now various designs of 'clean nose' karabiners where there is no lip where the gate locates itself for your wires or rope to snag on.

Different types of snapgate karabiners, alloy straight gate, alloy bent gate, wire gate and key locking (clean nose).

Gate chatter – Hit the back bar of a snap gate karabiner against your palm. The alloy gate will make a clicking sound if you do it hard enough (a wire gate won't). The open gate strength of a karabiner is marked on the side and is usually one third of the strength when the gate is closed. This is just one of the reasons why it is better to use screwgate karabiners in anchors and for important links.

As well as snapgate karabiners you will need a selection of screwgate kara-biners for attaching yourself to belays and your belay plate. They also come in a variety of shapes, sizes and designs. In general you'll need one HMS or oval karabiner for your belay plate, one large HMS for tying into belays and a couple of extra D-shaped karabiners as a bare minimum.

D-shaped, pear-shaped HMS, large HMS and mini-HMS screwgate karabiners.

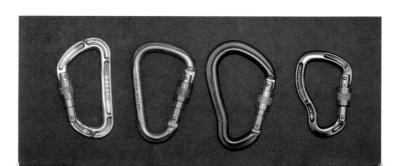

Wires (nuts or rocks)

You are better off buying wires that are common in the country where you climb (in the UK these are DMM, Clog and Wild Country). Their designs have altered little in years, and over that period many placements have become sculpted through having the same wires constantly placed in them.

Everybody has a different idea as to how many wires to take on a route. If you are climbing on a gritstone edge then the chances are you will be able to make a reasonable guess about the sizes you'll need and which it might be prudent to double up on. On longer and multi-pitch routes it is better to double up on all sizes of wires, and rack them accordingly, as you will not be able to see the whole route and may need a greater selection of gear.

A set of wires sizes 1 to 11. Wires, nuts, rocks, wedges? It's all crack protection.

This karabiner has been overloaded with wires, and will result in them getting tangled. Sod's law means it will happen when you least want it to. Worse still the wires might drop off mid route

How to rack even ten wires is a problem, as even this is too many for a single karabiner. To rack twenty, break them down into sets of small, medium and large with six or seven wires on each karabiner. It's best to have a small overlap in the sets; so if you were going to have a doubled up rack of wires from size 1 to 10, one way to break them down would be:

Small – size 1 x 2, size 2 x 2, size 3 x 2, size 4 x 1

Medium – size 4 x 1, size 5 x 2, size 6 x 2, size 7 x 1

Large – size 7 x 1, size 8 x 2, size 9 x 2, size 10 x 2

Racking up a double
set of wires on
three karabiners.

You could switch one of the size 10 wires for a size 11, giving you something slightly bigger. Wires now go all the way up to size 14, but you might have those sizes already covered by other large gear like Hexes or cams.

If you are going to have a double set of wires it is better to have one set of wires from one manufacturer and the other set of wires from another company. The sizes will be slightly different, giving you a wider choice.

*RPs are micro
wires named after
Roland Pauligk*

If the route requires micro wires, you can rack up to eight of these on a karabiner (with RPs it is sometimes easier to get a few more onto a karabiner, as long as you don't mind the odd tangle). How you rack these on your harness is up to you, but stay organised; all the wires on one side; or split small wires on one side, large on the other.

A range of micro wires.

A slider nut.

There is also a more specialist nut, called a slider; these are often good in very small, almost parallel sided cracks. Seldom used, often on routes where it is known to be the only available runner. As such it is mentioned only for completeness.

Hexes

Hexes are best threaded with spectra tape; it means that at a push you can clip the rope straight into the gear without a quickdraw. For this you will need one karabiner for each Hex. If you double or triple up Hexes on one karabiner, they are guaranteed to get in a tangle right when you need them.

A selection of DMM Torque Nuts, which have an extendable sling. They are a great alternative to Rockcentric Hexes.

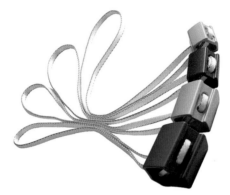

Choose your smallest Hex to be bigger than your largest wire and choose two more Hexes up to around a size 9 (three is a good quantity). Some people will carry more, others may carry none, preferring cams. Some rock types take Hexes better than cams (eg. some cracks on the sea cliffs at Gogarth, Wales are very irregular and take large Hexes in natural taperings).

Another type of semi-passive large crack protection which can be used in Hex placements is the Tri-cam (see page 30), which is one of the only reliable pieces of gear for quarried shot holes, but otherwise a rarity.

Cams

The range of active camming devices seems unfathomable, but not as complicated as you might think. There are three different types of camming device; the original single solid stem, the single flexible stem and the double flexible stem, all have pros and cons but they all do the same job.

DMM Dragon Cams and a few other manufacturers now have two or more axles on their cams, giving them a greater range between being fully open and full closed, so one cam will fit a greater range of cracks. If you are only going to have a couple of cams on your rack, multi-axled is a good idea.

A Trango double axle cam.

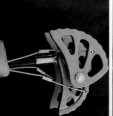
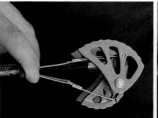

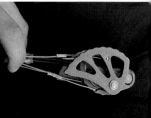

Cams provide protection in places that would otherwise be protectionless and although they need to be placed with care, once mastered they can be placed very quickly. The invention of the 'cam' helped to push back the frontiers in traditional rock climbing. On long routes, alpine climbs or big walls you will see climbers carrying a very expensive skirt of such devices from the smallest to the very largest.

Lightweight, comfortable to use and in quarter sizes the DMM range of cams offers an overlap between sizes.

Manufacturers like DMM and Wild Country now make their range of cams in quarter sizes, meaning that you have the biggest selection of sizes. On long routes, where you may place a lot of gear, such as on mountain routes, sea cliffs or big walls, this option of having lots of gear can pay dividends. If you only took a few multi-axled cams because they have a greater size range you might end up with nothing left to place, whereas with a large number of quarter sized cams you may still have a reasonable range left to choose from. This and the doubled over extension sling means that at a push you don't need to extend the cam.

A doubled over sling mean that, at a push, they don't need extending.

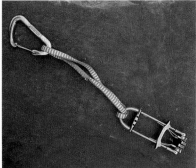

Which sizes should you take with you up a route? Look out for any wide cracks, or a route description or route name which suggests one. If it is all wide cracks do you need to take small cams? Starting out a new rack you should perhaps own sizes 1, 2 and 3 in camming devices if going for the more common single-axled cam. As your climbing develops you will notice what size cams would be most useful for the routes you are climbing.

The most important thing to remember about cams is that they can walk out of the placement you put them in if the rope moves the stem. Modern twin-stemmed cams have a doubled over sling to extend them, but it is often prudent and sometimes essential to use a quickdraw as well to add another point of articulation and prevent this from happening.

B

Quickdraws and extenders

(A) If the stem is moved by the rope the cam can 'walk' in the placement or fall out. (B) Extending the cam can reduce sideways pulling on the stem.

A deceptively simple piece of equipment, which is key to minimising rope drag. You'll want to carry enough extenders of the right length. Sport climbing quickdraws are very short slings for bolted routes where all the bolts are drilled in a straight line to the top. But when it comes to trad routes, nature has seldom aligned all the gear placements. We need to straighten the zig-zag of runners using longer quickdraws and extenders.

A variety of different length quickdraws will help you to reduce rope drag by straightening the path of the rope.

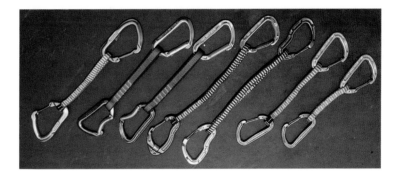

How to shorten a 60cm sling into a rapidly extendable quickdraw. To extend it unclip the rope from all but one bit of sling and pull, the sling will unfold.

You will need a set of at least eight quickdraws to begin with, for short routes. Of those you want some long (30cm), some medium (20cm) and a couple of short ones (15cm). It is also a good idea to have a sling shortened as an extender like this:

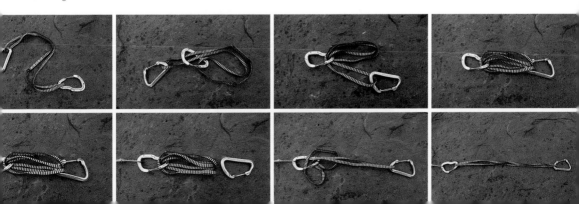

Carry a variety of slings both 60cm and 120cm, so you can extend gear a very long way if needed or use them on spikes as you pass. Keep your 120cm slings over one shoulder and across your body, held in place with a screwgate (see below) and your 60cm slings across the other shoulder to help prevent the slings tangling. Put your rucksack on before you shoulder your slings otherwise they will be stuck under the bag!

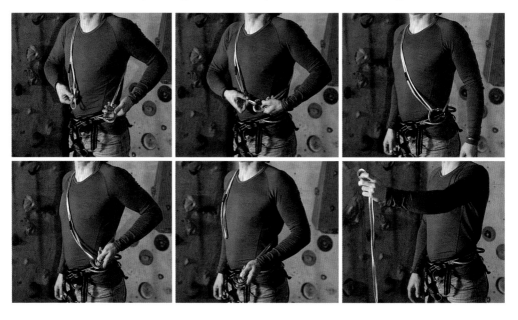

Rack 120cm slings by linking them with a karabiner. Then you can just undo the karabiner and remove the sling without taking it back over your shoulder.

When it comes to racking your quickdraws adopt a system that works for you. Some people have gear on one side and quickdraws on the other. Many leading climbers (because of the amount of equipment they carry) spread them out over all the gear loops.

Something to hold the karabiner for clipping the rope captive will help prevent it turning upside down (making it hard to clip). A bit of finger tape, an elastic band or castration ring can be used to captivate the karabiner. Some manufacturer's quickdraws have a stitched through retainer to hold the karabiner at one end. The captive karabiner determines which end to clip to the rope – some quickdraws are also colour coded (red to rope is easy to remember).

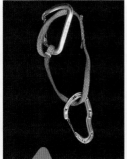

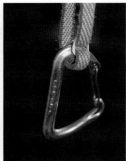
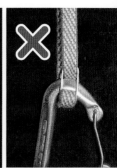

WARNING – If you use a sling as a quickdraw with an elastic band or similar to captivate one end, beware that if it gets tangled up in your bag and the sling clips itself through the karabiner, then there is a danger that when you untangle it the sling will look OK from one side, but is actually only held on by an elastic band. Check each quickdraw as you rack up.

Having one karabiner clearly defined as for the rope means that if you were to go sports climbing and take a few falls the karabiner that has been attached to the bolt may well suffer from scratches leaving potentially sharp edges. If you were to clip this damaged karabiner to the rope and fall you will probably damage your rope. Having one of the karabiners in a quickdraw captive will also help to identify which one clips to the rope.

This karabiner has been fallen on whilst sport climbing, and the bolt has damaged the inner surface of the karabiner. If this were clipped to the rope it may damage the sheath of the rope. Colour coded quickdraw – red for rope – helps to keep one end free of bolt damage.

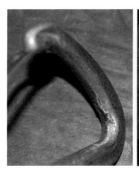
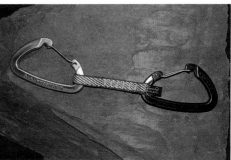

An improvised mini clip stick - the gripper clipper, if you need to stretch to clip in situ gear, one of these can be a god send. (Right) Some people carry a longer (up to 6m) clip-stick around with them, for clipping the bolts on a sports route, placing a first wire or brushing holds which are out of reach.

A tweak you may find useful when to make a move up to reach a bolt is too tenuous is to make a 'gripper clipper'. With some tape and your old toothbrush you can create one mini clip-stick to add to your rack.

Racking up tips (three example racks below)

1. A basic climbing rack for starting out on easy routes.

2. A more complex rack suitable for big mutli-pitch routes, where the rack is split small wires and small cams on one side, with large wires and large cams on the other.

3. Is exactly the same rack as in example two but all the wires are racked on one side and all the cams on the other. Not one of these examples are wrong, but one might work better for you than others.

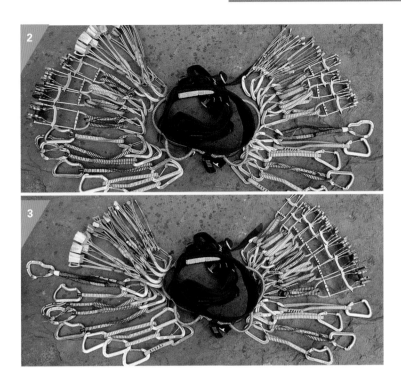

PLACING GEAR EFFICIENTLY

Effective placement of gear comes down to three things, knowing your racking system, developing a good eye for placements as well as the appropriate size of relative protection, and using rests where possible to place gear whilst in balance.

Finding a hands-off rest to place protection is a vital skill.

The first two are down to hands-on experience with your rack and gear placements. You might go through your racking system at home, trying to reach straight for the piece of gear you think of and take it off and replace it in the same position in time each time. Getting to know gear placements is down to time spent at the crag.

You can, however, practise the hands-off rests we covered earlier. By being in balance you avoid placing gear mid move in a strenuous position. You may find that the instant you have placed your runner you find a better position to place it from. Try to be relaxed when placing gear and ask yourself whether if you make another half move you will be in a more balanced position?

When at a rest it is sometimes possible to see a gear placement above. You may be able to judge the size from the rest, select the correct wire and clip it to a quickdraw ready to place, saving time and energy. Some people climb up with the gear ready in their mouths (but be careful not to drop it and metal plays havoc with your tooth enamel!)

Gear placement exercise – Rack up ready to climb and walk along the bottom of a cliff playing 'guess the placement'. Find a crack and guess the best size of gear. Experiment with other sizes to see if you have the best fit. See page 27 for tips on gear placement. You may be able to judge the size of a placement in finger widths; one finger = cam 1, two fingers = cam 2 and so on.

Placing gear on lead exercise – When you are leading try to place gear only where you can stand in balance or from a hands-off rest. Place the gear from here and before you leave this position take time to look up and spot the next rest and gear placement. Take the time to look at how you might climb the next section.

WARNING – Lead climbing is dangerous. Before attempting this exercise it is worth practising placing gear on your route whilst on a top rope, trailing a rope to simulate lead climbing. Make sure that your belayer has the necessary skill to stop you if you fall!

RISKY LEADS

As well as needing all the technical skills, lead climbing is an activity that requires us to carry out an ongoing assessment of the risks involved. It is a balancing act between the quality of your protection, the difficulty of the climbing, the potential for a fall and the consequences if you were to fall.

At times there may be a low chance of falling because the climbing is easy, but serious consequences if you were to fall. A steady and considered approach is needed to continue on such terrain as you are in the danger zone. At the other end of the spectrum the chance of falling is high but good gear may mean there will be no serious consequences. You can afford to be a little reckless with your movement as you are in the safe zone. Then there is the grey area that lies between the safe and the danger zone where it can be hard to recognise the true risk.

SINGLE VS DOUBLE ROPES

The features of single and double ropes.

Many climbers choose double ropes, but the decision to use a single or a double rope is not always simple.

Single rope	Double ropes
UIAA symbol for single rope ①	UIAA symbol for half ropes (½)
Approximate rope diameter – 9mm to 11mm	Approximate rope diameter – 7.5mm to 9mm
Easier to belay on one rope	Harder to belay two ropes simultaneously
Easier to hold a fall on one thicker rope	Harder to hold a fall on skinnier ropes
More likely to get rope drag	Less likely to get rope drag
Can only retreat half the length of the rope and retrieve the rope	Can retreat the whole length of the rope when the two ropes are joined together, and retrieve the ropes
Can be used on its own (ideal for indoor or sport climbing)	Have to be used in pairs (not very good for indoor or sport climbing)
Easy to use on a straight up route	Easy to use on a straight up route
Harder to manage the rope on a wandering vertical route or traverse	Easier to manage on a wandering vertical route or traverse
Higher impact force caused by not so stretchy thicker rope	Lower impact force caused by stretchier thinner ropes
Can leave the second with a nasty pendulum	Can help protect the second on some traversing sections

So far we have looked only at the using a single rope, but you may favour the versatility of double ropes as the pitches become longer and more sinuous. It goes without saying that controlling one rope is going to be easier than controlling two. Being able to pay out with one rope whilst taking in on another is something that you need to ensure your belayer can cope with.

Holding the live rope to pay out or take in (A) the blue rope and (B) the yellow rope. (C) Keeping control of both ropes in one hand.

Belaying with double ropes exercise – In a controlled environment like at the base of a crag, climbing wall or at home, attach your double ropes to your belay device and get a friend to ask randomly for slack on one rope, whilst you don't let any rope through on the other. Have two different colour ropes and ask for 'slack' on one colour, whilst not paying out on the other.

Once you are slick at this try taking in on one rope whilst not letting any of the rope out on the other.

Repeat this, but concentrate on not letting go of either dead rope at any time. Again once you are slick at this move onto trying to pay out with one rope whilst taking in on the other. Try this with both ropes and always have a hand on both dead ropes coming out of the belay plate.

WARNING – Your belayer needs to be able to belay competently with double ropes. Consider doing these exercises before you get on a testing lead, as well as starting out on a route that you will find easy so that the belayer can get used to handling two ropes simultaneously whilst you are not going to be in a life or death situation.

Different ways to manage a single and double rope on a wandering vertical route. Using long extenders may straighten the path of the rope, and double ropes make it even easier to run the rope straight. Note that at least one of the runners in the single rope example is being pulled upward (and potentially out!)

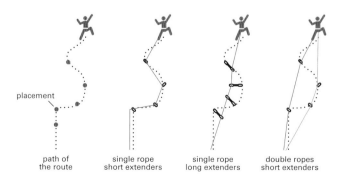

placement

| path of the route | single rope short extenders | single rope long extenders | double ropes short extenders |

Why do you need to be able to operate both ropes independently? There are times when the lead or second may need slack on one rope and rope taken in on the other. See the diagram below; the red rope is clipped to a runner above the climber's head, making a mini top rope on red, whilst still leading on blue. As they climb up the red rope needs to be taken in and the blue rope paid out.

It's necessary to take in and pay out the ropes independently. In step two the belayer needs to take in red whilst paying out blue.

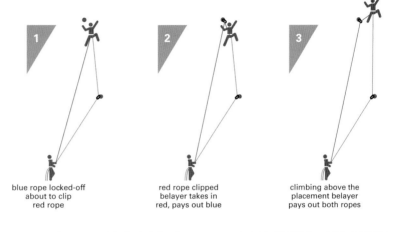

blue rope locked-off
about to clip
red rope

red rope clipped
belayer takes in
red, pays out blue

climbing above the
placement belayer
pays out both ropes

Two ways to use double ropes on the same route, both are OK. Although it is arguable that the first example is the better as it not reliant solely on one rope in different sections.

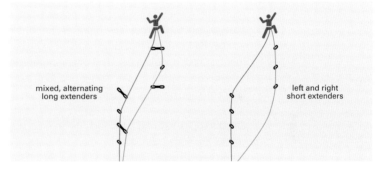

mixed, alternating
long extenders

left and right
short extenders

Bear in mind that with two skinny ropes standard belay plates are designed for thicker single ropes and won't provide as much friction when it comes to stopping a fall. Be aware of this and pay closer attention to the climber. With some modern super skinny ropes you may wish to consider a specifically designed belay plate like the DMM Buggette or Petzl Reversino.

Using a single rope, even if you use long quickdraws, can lead to an increase in rope drag. More changes of angle in the rope will also drag sideways or upward on your runners (which may be unseated from their placements and even lifted out). Look out for the line of the route and the position of your runners and use longer quickdraws or double ropes to reduce problems.

Double ropes require greater planning. From the ground look at your route with even more care to work out where the route climbs and where potential runners are. Try to project the straightest lines possible with two ropes, using different lengths of quickdraw. For wandering routes that climb predominantly vertically use your ropes as left and right; for traverses use your ropes as a high and a low; whilst on a perfectly straight up corner or crack it is possible to use either rope in alternate runners.

Ways to use double ropes on (A) a straight up crack/corner with alternate ropes clipped into runners, (B) a wandering vertical wall where one rope is clipped to runners on the left and the other on the right, (C) a traverse where one rope is clipped into high runners and the other lower runners.

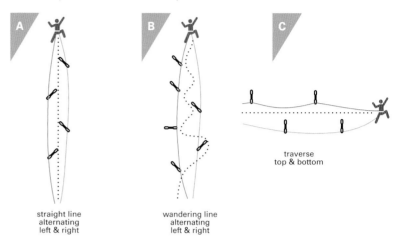

straight line
alternating
left & right

wandering line
alternating
left & right

traverse
top & bottom

As well as planning it is often necessary to adjust your plan whilst on the route; however the leader often doesn't get the complete picture. The belayer can sometimes see more of the whole pitch so may be able to advise the leader by encouraging them to clip a specific rope into the next runner. Often shouting up 'This runner on the pink rope' takes the pressure of decision making off the leader and lets them know that the second is concentrating on what is going on.

Double ropes have no advantage indoors or on sports climbs, because the routes are bolted with a single rope in mind and it can be harder to clip both ropes into a single quickdraw.

A final pitfall with double ropes is they often get twisted around each other. There is one way to avoid this; never turn around on a stance (this takes a great deal of concentration when you arrive at a belay). It is often possible to get rid of any twists before a climber seconds or leads off on multi-pitch climbs, by simply turning around the opposite way or passing one rope over your head and then stepping over it.

Mind Games

Llion Morris masters 'Ancient Art' in the Fisher Towers, Utah. This exposed pinnacle requires as much mental composure as physical prowess.

SELF EFFICACY

Previous Performance

Witness Experience

Verbal Persuasion

Arousal

increasing effect ↑

This section covers the basics of sport psychology, a growing field of academic research which is spreading light on this dark art of climbing. Confidence is one of the most important attributes for a lazy climber.

Self efficacy – your confidence at a task (climbing) when faced with the surroundings. Your confidence to complete a boulder problem may be totally different from your confidence lead climbing a trad or sports route at an equivalent grade of difficulty. The building blocks of self efficacy (left) include arousal, verbal persuasion, witness experience and previous performance.

Previous performance

Keeping a log of your routes over the years may reveal trends in your successes, failures and habits.

Previous climbing successes make us feel more confident we can achieve something equal or harder. If you climbed the route in good style rather than survived by the skin of your teeth, all the better. A steady build up of harder and more demanding routes can help us to come away with a positive experience. Route to route, day to day, week to week or year to year. The feeling of success is important to reflect on and recall at times when things get tough.

When we fail (it wouldn't be the challenge if we didn't) we need a robust belief in our ability to bounce back. Think rationally and find a positive experience in failure.

Most people fit between two categories: Pessimists who see failure as a reoccurring pattern (that extends into all areas of their climbing) and that failure is due to personal shortcoming and success down to luck; and optimists who view success as their own doing and failure as chance or an external influence, when any failure will be seen as an isolated event. Whichever type of personality you tend toward the best thing to be is rational in your expectations and thinking.

> **Previous performance exercise** – Start every climbing session with an easy warm-up route and build up to match or exceed your previous level through steady progression.

> Whether you succeed or fail, keep your thoughts rational.

> Use visualisation to recall the emotion and feelings that come with success and to remember your greatest climbs.

Witness experience

Learn from other people's mistakes, failures and successes. It is often easier to have a rational approach to other people's performances, because we are emotionally detached from the experience. Analysing other people's performances rationally will help you do the same for your own performance.

Lets say for example you are climbing with one or more friends and you know from previous experience that you can climb at the same level. Witnessing their success you will feel more confident in your own ability to succeed on the same route.

> **Witness experience exercise** – When climbing as a group of similar ability at a bouldering wall make an effort to let different people climb each problem first. Quite often you find the first person to climb the route will look less in control than those that follow. After someone has succeeded the chances are that everyone will succeed reasonably quickly.

Imagery

Related to witness experience is imagined experience, something many people do subconsciously. Like a physical technique, this mental skill can be developed through training.

You might imagine an individual move, a single route or entire day's climbing. By imagining the moves or the process of a day out climbing you will be warming up your brain for action, considering all the angles to eliminate surprises and creating the expectation of a positive outcome.

Imagery (the basics 1) – Start with something nice and simple; take a few deep breaths, close your eyes and relax.

Imagine yourself walking up your road towards your house, as you approach the door you reach your key to the lock, open it and enter through the door. As you walk into the house you head up the stairs and into your bedroom, and sit down on the bed.

What did you experience? Did you imagine the experience as if seeing it through you own eyes, or was it as if someone was filming a documentary of you? These perspectives are 'internal' and 'external imagery'. Was the scene silent or were there sounds, smells and sensations as you grasped the key or climbed the stairs? These aspects are 'kinaesthetic imagery'.

Try the exercise again and see if you pick up on any extra information.

Imagery (the basics 2) – Sit down and relax again. Imagine the colour blue, take a minute to explore the image you have.

What was it you imagined? A swimming pool, the sea, a nice blue sky or just the colour blue. Did this image conjure up any thoughts and feelings? Warm, cold, sunshine or winter. Everyone is different and there are no wrong or right answers, the important thing is what these images mean to you and how you experience them.

It helps to have a 'script' to focus your use of imagery and it takes practice to become good at it. The sequence of events you were talked through in the first imagery exercise (entering your house) was just such a 'script'. The current thinking is that up to 15 minutes a day is enough to develop your imagery and create a lasting effect.

Imagery script exercise – A script for something familiar, making a cup of coffee, this time using props. Read through the script, then using props (don't use a hot kettle, as you will have your eyes shut) run through the script. After that, actually make yourself a cup of coffee, before re-reading the script and then imagining it a final time.

Picking up the spoon you feel the cold stainless steel on your hand.

The smell of coffee reaches you as you delicately scoop a pile onto the spoon.

Tipping the spoonful of coffee into the cup you hear the granules bouncing off the china cup.

As you wait for the kettle to boil you hear the water bubbling away inside. The kettle turns itself off with a click and you watch the steam rise from the spout.

Pouring the water into the cup you feel the heat from the kettle on your hand, you hear the sound of the water filling the cup and you smell the aroma of the coffee.

Pouring a final splash of milk the drink is ready.

Taking a drink from the cup you taste the smooth coffee and feel the warmth in your stomach.

This process of imagining with props and then actually going through the process will help you to develop a more vivid image in your mind's eye.

Imagery with props – Devise a few imagery exercises yourself with climbing equipment to help you, e.g. clipping a karabiner or quickdraw; grasping a hold; belaying a top rope; making a belay.

Writing a script is straightforward. First you need a basic story that you want to imagine, then add some visual and kinaesthetic descriptions (these need to be positive and will play a part in self talk later). After that you then need to add actions and emotions. The final step is to refine your script into more flowing, brief paragraphs. Check out the example on the page 164.

Imagery script for entire day – As well as visualising entire routes, it is also possible to construct positive daydreams of entire situations. Take a day out sea-cliff climbing.

Maybe read aloud your script and record it. Listening to a recording of yourself has been demonstrated to improve your imagined experience.

Sit down and relax, take a minute to slow your breathing and let any tension in your body subside. Start to visualise the next day. The sun is rising and breaks through the curtains. Finishing the first cup of coffee of the day you start to sort through your rack; see yourself meticulously sorting through it and checking that all the cams are working smoothly. Feel yourself packing your rack into your rucksack and hear the metal jangle. Waiting for your climbing partner to call, you feel excited at the day ahead.

See yourself in the car driving to the cliff, the views and smells that you experience along the way. You arrive in the car park, taking the bags out of the car and feeling their weight as you shoulder them. See yourself standing tall as the rucksack seems weightless to you now. Listen to the sound of your feet crushing the gravel as you walk into the cliff, feel the sun and wind on your smiling face as you contemplate a perfect day cragging.

As you arrive at the racking up spot, feel yourself taking a few deep breaths and admire the view. You rack up listening to the sea birds and the sound of the sea. Absorb every ounce of the situation. You rig the abseil and see yourself confidently abseiling down, enjoying the excitement of the situation.

As you start to make the belay at the bottom of the cliff, feel the tension release from your head to your toes. Watch the sea birds sore above, the waves crashing below; there is no better place to be than here.

See yourself leaving the belay. Looking up at the climb ahead you can see the way to go and it looks easy. Watch yourself climbing, feel the rock under your fingers and every hold feels like a massive ledge. Watch yourself picking the exact size wire for every placement, the feeling of relaxation as each bomber runner is clipped effortlessly into the rope.

At the belay you clip yourself into your bomber anchor, feeling the wind in your hair as you sit back on the belay and start to bring up the second. The birds fly past admiring your belay and the sea has become a distant friend, lapping in and out at the foot of the cliff below. As you watch the waves billow in and out, you notice that it is in time with your breathing.

As you lead off on the last pitch you know the route is in the bag, every part of your body feels strong. As you stand below the final wall you take the time to look back at where you have been, the sights, the sounds and the feel of the rock under your hands. Success is near, you take one last deep breath and commit to the final moves.

As you feel the top hold, you confidently move your foot up and perform a perfect mantel onto the top of the cliff. The final push up brings the feeling of elation and success. You have not just climbed the route but enjoyed every part of it. It was the best climb of your life. As you bring up the second you reflect on every part of the day, as the sun warms your face and a gentle breeze ruffles your hair.

Step1: Basic story	**Step2:** Adding emotion and detail		**Step 3:** Refined script
Preparing to climb	**Excited, nervous, confident, relaxed, prepared**	Sat down on the bouldering mat I feel nervous but excited, squeaking my boots clean I feel prepared and ready to go.	Sat down on the bouldering mat I feel nervous and excited as I rub my boots clean until they squeak under my thumb. Chalking up my hands I start to prepare.
Focus on success	**Relaxed, concentration**	Slowing down my breathing I feel myself relax, and tension leave my body as I concentrate on the finishing jug.	Taking a few deep and cleansing breaths I relax and let any tension leave my body as I concentrate of the finishing jug.
Stepping onto the problem	**Rough holds, grip of fingers, pressure on feet, muscular tension, readiness**	Gripping the rough holds, feel the grip of the fingers and the tension return to just the right muscles in readiness to climb.	As I take hold of the starting holds I feel the rough grip under my fingers, and the tension start to build in just the right muscles in readiness to climb.
Flowing movement	**Swing of body, flow of movement, fluid, ease, relaxed, determined**	Ascending feel body swing effortlessly and with ease between the holds in a determined fashion, with fluid like sensation.	Pulling myself off the ground I ascend feeling my body swinging effortlessly from hold to hold, there is a fluidity to my movement as I ease myself between the holds in a determined fashion.
Cruising the crux	**Set up, focus, power, strength, body position, controlled aggression**	Setting up for the crux, I focus on the body position and wind up all my power and strength ready to unleash them with control aggression.	Setting up for the crux, I focus on the foot holds and body position, as I wind up all my power and strength like a coiled spring, ready to unleash it with controlled aggression.
Holding the finishing jug	**Determined, relaxed, focused, breathe, reach, grasp**	Through the crux my mind focuses on the finishing jug, as I breathe a relaxing breath and make the final determined reach to grasp the final hold.	Above the crux, my mind focuses on the finishing jug, as I take a relaxing breath before the final determined reach to grasp the final hold. Latching the last hold a feeling of contentment and pride washes over me, as the success sinks in.

Useful steps for writing your own script.

Mental rehearsal

Watching video of yourself can enhance the vividness of your imagery. Editing together or overlaying video segments of film to make it look as if you completed a route successfully will help you to imagine success and has been demonstrated to improve performance.

Mental rehearsal is a very similar technique to imagery, which is useful when trying to redpoint a route or boulder problem you have tried before. You will be able to call on your experience to address the specifics of that route or boulder problem. Many top climbers report visualising hard routes in day and night dreams, as well as part of the final preparation just before they set off on an attempt.

It is also of use when trying to onsight routes by allowing you to virtually climb the route or boulder problem before you step off the ground. Your ability to read moves from the ground is important, otherwise you might practise the move incorrectly during your rehearsal (it is useful to run through several options if you are unsure).

Watching yourself climb on a video or digital camera can help you visualise the route. You could even film a series of overlapping moves from a climb and then edit them together to make it look like you actually climbed the route. Anything which might help you to imagine the result that you are trying to achieve.

Mental rehearsal exercise – Visualise yourself stood at the bottom of a route. This could be internally or externally, but most importantly try and include some kinaesthetic imagery as well.

Looking up, think about how you are going to climb the route, where you are going to put your hands and feet as you step off the ground, what the rock will feel like. As you climb in your mind, what does each move look and feel like? See yourself cruising through the crux, calmly placing the crucial runners, swiftly clipping the rope into every quickdraw, confidently making the final moves to the belay and the feeling of success when stood at the top of a well executed pitch.

Why does visualisation work?

Viewing yourself in the 'third person', as if being filmed, helps to ready your mind for the activity and considering every move helps to eliminate surprises. It can also help you to turn a potentially negative experience into an entirely positive one; instead of anxiety you can choose to visualise the crux move with a feeling of excitement. By viewing yourself in the third person you become emotionally detached from the situation you find yourself in and you are better able to examine the real situation that you might find yourself in when climbing.

Visualising the moves fires up the premotor cortex in the frontal lobe of your brain, an area involved in the sensory guidance of movement. Your brain does everything other than making the muscles move. Get a friend to visualise a boulder problem and you will be able to feel their muscles twitch as they think about the moves. As well as this passive practice, visualisation allows you to experience the route without failure (a persistent point of failure may have become a mental block).

Visualisation top tips

Needs to be practised – up to 15 minutes a day.

External with kinaesthetic imagery is best, but some people will find it hard to imagine this – it is best to use what you feel confident with.

Use props and video to help develop the vividness of imagery.

Visualisation can be passive (sat down and still) or dynamic (stood up and moving). Dynamic imagery helps encourage kinaesthetic feelings.

Use scripts specific to your needs (redpoint routes, emotional response, anxiety control, improving confidence).

Verbal persuasion

Verbal persuasion is another of the building blocks of self-efficacy. Persuasion can come from many sources, usually your climbing partners. Anything you say to the people you are climbing with can have a positive or negative effect on their climbing. Most importantly verbal persuasion needs to be rational; it would be both dangerous and unacceptable to encourage someone to continue up a route if they are likely to fail in a dangerous situation (a difficult decision for any onlooker to make).

If you have a negative effect on someone's climbing it won't be long before they figure it out and start climbing with someone who gives them confidence. Quite often it is only small things that you may say that plants a seed of self doubt. Consider what positive words of encouragement you use and congratulate people on their accomplishments, however jealous you are.

As a belayer you need to be able to put yourself in the shoes of the leader, and think what would be going on in your mind in that situation; try to think of ways in which you can counteract negative thoughts and build positive ones. As an onlooker you will be more emotionally detached from the situation and better placed to rationalise doubts or fears the leader may have.

If you think the leader is having a nervous minute, ask them how things are going, listen to the reply and see if there is any way you can rephrase and reframe the thoughts of the leader to rationalise the situation and turn negatives into positives.

"The gear is bad" ➔ "The last runner below that was a good one".

"The move is impossible" ➔ "Shake out on that rest, relax for a while then have another look".

"This looks pumpy" ➔ "It looks like the gear is good, and if you climb quickly it slabs off, so you'll soon reach a good rest above".

"It's really bold" ➔ "You've done alright so far, relax on those holds for a moment and then take it nice and steady to the top".

"I'm scared" ➔ "The gear's just below your feet and it's good, take a few deep breaths, calm down and then see how things look".

Self talk

We have an internal chatter which goes on in our mind almost all the time. Some days that inner voice will be telling us to be cautious and at other times it is ready for a fight with a harder route. Sometimes we have a very positive attitude and will be better at facing our demons as we climb. At other times when we are down our inner chatter will reflect this. There will be days when we can 'go for it' and others when we can't. The important thing is to recognise what type of day it is today.

It is possible to concentrate on positive thoughts. These might not necessarily be outcomes, but about the process. Whilst stood at the bottom of a long route it may not be possible to say to yourself "I am going to succeed", but instead looking up you might be able to say with more confidence, "I can make it to that ledge/gear/groove" (important when breaking down a route).

Above all avoid negative words like 'fall', 'fail', 'pressure' and 'impossible'. Instead use positive words and sentences, but be rational; if a runner is poor then perhaps concentrate on the runner below that or a good ledge or placement above.

"I can do this" – not "I can't".

"This looks OK" – not "this looks impossible".

"I am going to succeed" – not "I am not going to fail".

"The gear is excellent" – not "the gear is OK".

"I will give it 110%" – not "I can't do this" or "its too hard".

"I might succeed" – not "I might fall off".

"I feel great" – not "I feel OK".

Sometimes you may need to alter your approach, so whilst a steady ascent may get you through 90% of the climb, the crux might need you to climb explosively. Your body may be willing but your mind may not be. Have ready some cue words that quell negative thoughts and help you commit. These cue words may start off as a phrase (or even a song) and become abbreviated. "Power through the crux" or "Go for it", becoming "Power" or "Go".

Similarly you can associate a phrase like "Chill out" or "Relax" with a relaxation exercise as a short cut to a relaxed state. Mark Twight in his book Extreme Alpinism talks of using the sound of a clicking karabiner in conjunction with relaxation, so the 'click' induces a relaxed emotional response.

Identifying negative self talk – We are often unaware of our negativity. Focus on your self talk by clicking a karabiner or move it from one gear loop to another every time you have a negative thought. When you top out or return to the ground, write down in a notebook all those thoughts along with when and where on the route you experience each one.

You'll have to repeat this exercise several times to get an idea of a pattern of thoughts that reoccur. Then devise a strategy to intervene every time a negative thought occurs by replacing it with a new phrase or cue word.

Self talk cue words exercise – If you hesitate on the crux of routes, or get ledge fever on routes and need something to get you going try finding a cue word. Invent a phrase like "Go for it" and use it every time you are about to embark on a hard sequence. By using that phrase on every route you will eventually associate it with committing totally to a crux.

It is not just positive words that help promote an optimistic outlook. Physical factors, emotions and arousal all play a part. Your body posture reflects your mood and your mood is affected by your posture. By altering your posture you can alter your mood. At the same time as saying "I can do this", straighten your back, bring your shoulders back and head up – you are going to succeed. Think positively and have a positive posture.

If we are down emotionally and demotivated we may well have negative thoughts and feel physically tired. By altering our physical state by eating and moving about and by imagining going climbing, we can alter our mood and become motivated. All common sense, but being aware of this can help you make changes.

The environment and events around you affect everything you do, but your mood, thought, behaviour and physical state (body) also affect each other. By changing one you can improve another. Be aware of how you tend to react and you may be able to turn things to your advantage.

Arousal

Staying relaxed is an integral part of lazy climbing, which is often harder than you think. Exposure and environment conspire against you, a long run-out from the last runner can inspire a tangible feeling of fear. We can counteract these negative feelings but first we need a clear understanding of our limitations. Overcome your mental block to achieve what you are capable of but know when you are asking your body to do the impossible. Continually pushing your grade to climb harder is dangerous territory; crossing the line in the sand and redrawing it at your physical and mental limits can often backfire.

Things can get on top of you and all the hard work and effort can lead to you climbing worse than ever; this is the 'catastrophe effect'.

The performance catastrophe effect (from Hardy and Fazey 1987).

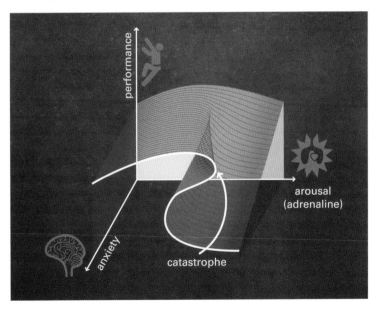

There are two main types of arousal in climbing; cognitive arousal (anxiety) and physiological arousal (the perceived effects of adrenaline). Everybody is different; some people will suffer more from anxiety, others show more physiological symptoms. How we interpret these feelings is important as the more negative our perception the more negative the effects.

Anxiety and failure

What might cause this drop in performance? It may be down to the volume of information the brain can deal with (the 7+/-2 chunks of information we can process get taken over by our worries and physiological arousal diverts our attention towards threats). It might force us to apply more effort or grip and become inefficient, or it may interrupt our subconscious skills and we revert to becoming a novice climber, thinking each and every movement through. Or it may be an 'ironic effect' – by thinking 'don't fall off!', we increase the likelihood of falling off.

Try this anxiety questionnaire – Read the statements in the table below (phrases climbers have used to describe their feelings before a climb). Circle the appropriate number to the right to indicate how you feel right now about your chosen route. There are no wrong or right answers.

Questionnaire developed by Dr Lew Hardy, SSHES, Bangor University.

	Not at all	A little	Moderate	Strongly	Very strongly
1 I feel jittery	1	2	3	4	5
2 I'm worried I may not be able to make the crux moves	1	2	3	4	5
3 I feel my heart beating rapidly	1	2	3	4	5
4 I am nervous	1	2	3	4	5
5 I feel I might not climb this route as well as I should	1	2	3	4	5
6 I have sweaty palms	1	2	3	4	5
7 I worry about failing on the route	1	2	3	4	5
8 I feel physically tense	1	2	3	4	5

9 I worry that I may not be able to find the right line	1	2	3	4	5
10 I feel anxious	1	2	3	4	5
11 I worry about falling	1	2	3	4	5
12 I have an underlying sense of uneasiness	1	2	3	4	5

Score the questionnaire for anxiety (even numbered questions) and arousal (odd numbered questions). Add the two scores for each set of six questions. 6 to 12 is a low score, 24 to 30 is high score. If you score highly in one of the forms of anxiety and you feel that it has a negative effect on your climbing then work on a coping strategy.

High anxiety is best countered with self-talk (cue words and counter arguments for the negative thoughts that you find yourself over analysing). Use imagery scripts to refocus images of failure on success.

High arousal is best countered with relaxation (mediation or breathing techniques to calm the effects of adrenaline). Whilst some relaxation techniques are great at home they are impractical whilst climbing. It is still important to practise relaxation, as staying relaxed is a key component to climbing at your limit and the more you practise controlled relaxation the easier you will be able to call on it at the crag. As you practise you will find yourself able to return to a relaxed state more quickly, as the relaxed mental state returns so will relaxed climbing.

It might take ten or more sessions to learn to relax in a short period of time (20–30 seconds).

Relaxation exercise (at home) – Either sitting up or lying down tense and then relax the muscles throughout your body up towards your head. Tense the muscles in your feet for 10 seconds and then slowly relax them, feel the sensation. Then move up to the legs, bottom, stomach; hands, arms, chest, shoulders, neck and face. Concentrate on the feeling that you have as you relax the muscles and focus on slow, steady breathing.

Relaxation exercise (at the crag) – Great just before setting out on a route. After preparing to climb by racking up, concentrate on areas of your body that feel tense. Move through your whole body tensing and then slowly relaxing the parts of your body that feel tight. As you move through the body, concentrate on the new relaxed feeling that enters the previously tense muscles. By the end of the exercise you should feel more relaxed, so focus on the route. Your level of anxiety will decrease as you relax.

Alternative relaxation exercise – For some people these exercises won't work. An alternative is to close your eyes and breathe slowly and deeply. Feel the tension in your head and neck as you breathe in and out. Then start to release that tension by visualising it leaving your body as a colour when you breathe out. As you breathe in see a soothing light enter your body and relax the tension in that part of the body. As you breathe work around your body releasing any tension you feel with each cleansing breath.

Relaxation exercise (whilst climbing) – At times you will find yourself tensing up and becoming anxious on a route; this is a common feeling. Concentrate on finding a nice stable position, preferably a hands-off rest. Then try and relax the tension in your arms, at the same time concentrate on slowing your breathing down. Breathe in through the nose and out through the mouth. Use a mantra like 're-' (as you breathe in) 'lax' (as you breathe out).

As you start to relax, use the rest to stretch out your forearms and relax them. Concentrate on the feeling of the muscles as you relax. Next shake out either arm above your head and then out to the side; this should allow you to stretch muscles in the shoulder, again concentrating on the feeling of relaxing the muscles after the stretch. (Shaking out your arms will also reduce the build-up of the pump.)

Focus on a small area of rock or a piece of gear. Look at it as you relax, examine it intensely, look at every crystal and feature of the rock. As you become more relaxed start to widen your focus, to the next handhold, then the next foothold. When you are fully relaxed you will be ready to take in a wider view and continue on your way.

Focus

It is possible to be too relaxed, you also need focus. A narrowing of the mind's eye, shutting out worries and concerns, concentrating all of your energy on the job in hand. There are many tricks to increasing your focus (sometimes referred to as the 'zone' when 100% focused on the activity).

Focus exercise 1 – Every time someone talks to you at work, school or socially, clear your mind and focus on that person and what they are saying. Let distractions fade away. Try transferring your focus to different things, from one conversation between friends to another and back again. See how long you can hold that focus before you change your attention. Work on holding your focus for longer and longer periods, you can even try it with objects on your desktop at work or coffee table at home.

Focus exercise 2 – Standing at the bottom of a route or boulder problem, start to visualise yourself climbing the line. As you visualise the moves, start to eliminate unnecessary distractions. Let the rock either side of the route blur out of focus, turn the volume down on the background noise, look to the top and focus in on the image of yourself topping out. When you feel ready start to climb.

Slack line walking exercise – Slack lines are great for developing focus, reactive balance and staying relaxed. Just have a go and as you improve you will feel your ability to remain focused and stay relaxed improve, along with your balance.

The warrior approach

Climbing at your limit is never easy (if you find it easy you probably aren't fulfilling your potential). At times a single pitch can feel like a battleground and it will take some grit and determination, not to mention courage, to succeed. See yourself as a rock warrior, a champion, hero or heroine.

Feel the energy and psyche building up at the bottom of a route you are about to unleash yourself on, the route stands no chance. If you want to, add a badly dubbed sound track and some Bruce Lee sound effects. When you feel sufficiently hyped up, focused and determined start up the route, attack it with all the cunning and guile of the lazy style of climbing you have learnt and when necessary unleash the fury.

A pre-climbing ritual

A simple four step approach to mental preparation at the bottom of the route. One of the attributes associated with elite sports people is a pre-competition routine, I am not talking about lucky pants, but a series of events like putting on your harness, racking up, tying in. Every time you go climbing follow the same routine, beginning with focusing on the route and relaxing. Eventually the focus and relaxation that you have associated with the process will occur almost automatically.

Prepare – Vanquish – Focus – Succeed

Prepare – for the route. Read the route description, put your harness on, rack up, tie into the rope, open your chalk bag, clean your boots till they squeak. Check everything twice. You are now as prepared as you can be.

Vanquish – all your demons. You have tied in properly, your harness is on right and you have checked twice, the belayer is all set, the gear is all racked just how you like it, your boots are clean so that they stick to the rock and you know where the route goes. There is nothing more you can do, you have answered all the questions in your mind.

Focus – on the route. Break it down into sections, look for the gear, and start to shut out the worry of the real world. That overdraft, those final demands, relationship worries or work stress can't be fixed on the rock face so leave them at home or tucked into your shoes with your socks.

Succeed – Commit to the route 100% of your ability and you will succeed.

FEAR OF FALLING

Imagery, self talk and relaxation exercises can all help a fear of falling. A more radical form of preparation, clip-drop training, can help to desensitise you – taking progressively longer and longer falls until you're happier with falling. The belayer needs to be safe and confident, you may even consider backing them up to start with. You'll also need an appropriate place to practise, indoors on an overhanging wall, dropping from the penultimate bolt (so that there will be a lot of energy absorbing rope out). If you are tempted to do this outdoors then remember that gear can fail, so think about making a mini belay at the high point, rather than using just one runner. Make sure the fall zone doesn't have any ledges you might hit.

Imagery techniques were first used clinically to treat phobias, with some success.

Imagery and relaxation – Relax, using one of the relaxation techniques from page 171 and imagine failing at the crux and falling (or any other fearful situation). With practice, eventually you will begin to associate the fearful stimuli with being relaxed rather than anxious.

Clip-drop exercise – The trick to using the clip-drop method described above is to make it progressive. The first time you fall, have the bolt clipped above your shoulders, warn the belayer and then jump off. Progress by falling with the bolt clipped level with your chest, then belly button, then waist, then thighs, then knees, then ankles until eventually you fall with the bolt below your feet. If you don't feel ready to progress, then don't. Get used to falling from where you feel comfortable. You may find you never take a practice fall with the bolt below your feet.

The trick is to regularly use some form of falling during your training session, this way you stay familiar with the feelings that falling evokes. When you are used to falling in a controlled situation, move on to routes at the limit of your ability so you are perhaps taking falls unexpectedly during your training.

Training: Basic Principles

(Above) A Bachar
ladder (designed by the
bouldering and training
genius John Bachar) is
a simple inclined rope
ladder, anchored at the
top and the bottom
with large wooden
rungs equally spaced.

*For most people in the
UK training for climbing
is an indoor activity;
remember that training
outside counts as well!*

The hardest part of training is
making the decision to start
training at all

– Wolfgang Güllich

If you have no reason to train, where are you going to find the motivation to continue a few months down the line? Many climbers will aimlessly rattle through the various training regimes and programmes never wishing to take on the challenge of long-term development. Others will pick and choose exercises from various sources and dabble with training.

Your training needs will be determined by your weaknesses and your goals. There is no panacea that will make you better in a matter of weeks, it often takes years of hard work to reach your potential and quite often a fair amount of pain. The exercises here are a guide to training for climbing in general and how to spot and strengthen your weaknesses.

THE WEAKEST LINK

A chain is only as strong as its weakest link. You may have strong arms, steely fingers and the highest blood oxygen throughput of anyone you know, but without good use of your feet and body position you are going to be climbing way below your potential, getting burnt off by weaker but more technical climbers. So skill is paramount. Just following a physical training regime won't lead to success. You need to identify what are **your** weak links and work to improve them. Developing your strengths will do no good because the weakest link will remain your breaking point.

Identifying your weaknesses – Examine your successes and compare them to your failures. Be honest. Draw two columns on some notepaper and label them, strengths and weaknesses.

List the routes/problems you failed on and also those you succeeded in doing. Successes under 'strengths' and failures under 'weaknesses'. Think about each route and note the reason you believe you failed. Ask a climbing partner what they believe were the weaknesses which led to your failed attempts. Is there a pattern amongst the style of route, angle, length, rock type or type of move?

Ask friends and climbing partners what they think your strengths and weaknesses are. Having watched you climb they may be a better judge than you.

Ask yourself if there is a type of rock, route or style of climbing that you don't enjoy. Add these to your list of weaknesses. Often we don't enjoy things as much if we don't excel at them. Add the style of routes you do enjoy to your list of strengths.

Review your list, does it seem right? Are there any other weaknesses that you feel you need to work on? Refine it to a short list of weaknesses (and strengths).

A much more robust approach to identifying your weaknesses is called 'performance profiling', a systematic approach which will help you identify not only physical weaknesses but tactical, technical and mental ones.

Performance profiling – Draw a table with four columns. In the first column note the physical attributes that form a solid base in your climbing be it strength, technique, etc. In the second column list attitudes you need to perform well and in the third list psychological skills that climbing requires. Then in the final column list the tactics you need in climbing. For example:

Physical	Attitudinal	Psychological	Tactical
Strength	Will to win	Confidence	Reading routes 15
Flexibility	Confidence 9	Overcoming fear 4	Jump for holds 18
Stamina 1	Positiveness	Self belief 14	Efficiency of movement
Arm strength 5	Competitiveness	Concentration 13	Finding rests
Finger strength 8	Liking challenges	Focus	Watching others
Shoulder strength 7	Determination 10	Confidence	Preparing for route 17
Leg strength	Desire to improve	Visualisation 19	
Power	Motivated	Imagery	
Core strength 2	Rising to challenge 20	Goal setting	
Balance 11	Discipline 12	Emotional control	
Technique 2	Single mindedness	Relaxation	
Footwork 6	Dedication	Cope with pressure	
Recovery time	Happiness	Cope with worrying thoughts	
Co-ordination	Aggression		
Endurance 3			
Weight control			

Once you have made a note of all the aspects you can think of, number the 20 most important on the list. Then transfer these to another table (see the example below). In a column next to each write a brief description, then in the next column add a rating of what the 'ideal climber' or 'climber you aspire to be' would score on a 1 to 10 scale. Alongside this rate your own current level. Subtract your score from the score of the ideal climber – the difference between you and where you want to be. Select the five areas of greatest difference and you have five areas to work on and set more specific goals.

Quality	Meaning	Ideal climber	Me	Difference
Stamina	Being able to climb for a long time	10/10	7/10	3
Arm strength	Bicep strength	9	8	1
Finger strength	Finger strength	10	7	3
Shoulder strength	Shoulder strength	10	8	2
Core strength	Ability to engage core stomach muscle and hold body tension	8	7	1
Balance	Maintaining a stable position	10	8	2
Technique	To use movement efficiently	10	6	(4)
Footwork	Using my feet	10	8	2
Confidence	Being confident in my abilities	10	7	3
Determination	A strong desire to succeed	10	6	(4)
Discipline	Sticking to training or climbing plans	10	8	2
Concentration	Focus on the climb, ignoring distractions	10	7	3
Visualisation	Imagining myself climbing	10	7	3
Endurance	Ability to carry on when pumped	10	7	3
Reading routes	Breaking the route into bite size chunks	10	6	(4)
Jumping for holds	Having the confidence to jump when you know you will fall off	10	6	(4)
Preparation	Thinking about the route before climbing.	10	6	(4)
Overcoming fear	Being able to relax and make good decisions.	8	6	2

Example of how to rate your ideal climber versus yourself in order to find the five most important factors to work on to improve your climbing. The scores highlighted in red are the most important factors to work on.

GOAL SETTING

Set your goal too high and you face disappointment, too low and you will not feel challenged and determined to progress. The type of goal you set is important, a dream or outcome goal like climbing a big wall in Yosemite will provide ongoing motivation but the dream alone will not help you. You need goals for the steps along the way that will lead you to your dream.

Having identified your weakness, set goals that develop those areas. For each weakness make a brief statement of what you will set out to achieve, any obstacles you might face on the way, the activities you will use and how long you will take to reach your goal. Make your goals **SMART** goals:

Attainable and Realistic – so important they said it twice in this acronym.

Specific | Measurable | Attainable | Realistic | Timed

How do you come up with some activities which will help you reach your goal? Try drawing a mind map.

A mind map of the things I need to do to help me climb E1.

A goal setting mind map – In the centre of the page write your dream goal, your final destination. Surround your dream with the five skills from your performance profile, each linked by a line. Break those five skills down into smaller chunks if you can, clustered around and each connected by a line.

Then consider what you can do to develop those skills. There may be just one activity, but it is best to try and think of at least three things you can do. Use the exercises described in this book to help fill in more activities. Link each activity back to each goal. You should be left with a web of activities, training requirements and skills you need to make it to your central goal.

Process goals vs outcome goals

Whilst an **outcome** goal like climbing E1 is great, what we really need are **process** goals, each of the parallel improvements needed to reach that outcome or dream. Process goals are far better at helping you to adhere to a training regime, as each process can be looked at separately, and allow you to measure your progress towards your outcome goals. Typical climbing process goals are improved strength, more efficient clipping, route reading, staying calm and refining areas of good technique.

Keep your performance profile, goal setting sheet and mind map so that you can monitor your progress, highlight new goals or decide to start over again with a better idea of what you need to do. Over the course of your training add to or alter your mind map. Know your weaknesses so you can address them; know the route you need to take to succeed; monitor your progress along the roads to success. The key is to ensure that all roads converge on the goal at the same time.

BASIC TRAINING

Hopefully you will have realised that there is more to climbing than simply being strong. The beauty of climbing is that success is the sum of many parts; technique, tactics, mental approach, physical ability and safety. So how do we improve our physical ability, the overall fitness of our bodies as a climbing machine? This machine is built up of nine major components, which themselves are built up of smaller parts. Work on all of these parts, bringing them to the same standard.

Nine essentials to the fitness engine

Strength – Our muscles' ability to exert a force against a resistant force, in climbing this is typically gravitational forces on our body mass.

Explosive strength (power) – The ability of our muscles to exert a force quickly in an explosive movement.

Agility – Our ability to make a series of explosive moves in any direction.

Balance – Our ability to keep our weight over our feet whilst still or moving.

Flexibility – The effective range of movement of our joints and limbs.

Local muscle endurance – A single or small group of muscles' ability to do sustained work.

Cardio vascular endurance – Our heart's ability to deliver oxygen to the muscles in the body and their ability to use it.

Power endurance – A muscle's ability to make near maximum contraction time after time.

Coordination – Our ability to combine all of these components to move effectively and efficiently.

Your metabolism

There is a chemical reaction within our muscles; stores of energy are used with every contraction and are replenished.

The fuel in our muscle cells is ATP (adenosine triphosphate) which, when it is spent, is converted into ADP (adenosine diphosphate). The blood flowing to the muscle replenishes the muscle by supplying the means to convert the ADP back into ATP, allowing the muscles to contract again.

The simple model of our muscle's fuel cycle. Gaining and losing a phosphate (P) group.

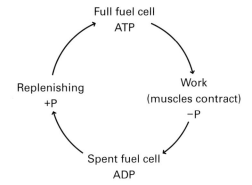

There are three ways that the body converts ADP back into ATP. Each way has it's pros and cons in terms of intensity, speed, length of contraction, the duration of exercise and the ability to continue working or reaching a point of failure.

The body's energy systems

Short intense climbing calls upon phosphocreatine and anaerobic systems.

Phosphocreatine – is stored in the blood and within the muscle cells and is very good at sharing its phosphate to convert ADP (adenosine diphosphate) back to ATP (adenosine triphosphate). Stored in the muscles it is instantly ready to use. It can operate at a high intensity of activity but only for a short period of up to 10 seconds. This system is called upon when we first exert ourselves until other systems kick in.

Aerobic respiration – is what we use the majority of the time. The free flow of oxygenated blood to the muscles allows the body to convert ADP to ATP. There are two energy sources the body uses aerobically; carbohydrates in the blood, muscles and liver, which is used between 60–80% of our maximum effort; and fat, which can only be used if we are working at a lower level of intensity of up to 40%. Supplying more oxygen to our muscles improves our aerobic ability. Our maximum supply of oxygen to the muscles that need it as measured as our 'VO$_2$ max'.

Climbing a short route at the limit of your ability will rely on your anaerobic endurance.

Anaerobic respiration – without enough oxygenated blood lactic acid is produced as a by-product of the conversion from ADP to ATP. It usually starts to occur when we reach 80% of our maximum effort, as well as in the first few seconds of activity after our phosphocreatine is exhausted. The intensity of activity at which the anaerobic respiration kicks in is referred to as our OBLA level (onset of blood lactate accumulation). As lactic acid builds up in our muscle we become pumped and we can only continue that level of exercise for a matter of minutes before we reach failure. As anaerobic respiration takes a few seconds to kick in; it complements the fast but short lived phosphocreatine system.

(A) Bouldering (intense bursts of climbing lasting up to two minutes) will rely on the phosphocreatine and anaerobic systems, with the aerobic system aiding recovery.

(B) Short intense single pitches (intense climbing lasting over two minutes) will call mainly on the anaerobic system with the aerobic system helping out when it can.

(C) Long sustained pitches (sustained climbing lasting up to one hour) will rely more on the aerobic system with the anaerobic system called upon to overcome the harder sections and aid your ability to recover.

(D) Long multi-pitch climbs (sustained climbing lasting hours) will be reliant on the aerobic system, although the anaerobic system will be called upon at the crux moves.

Each of these systems ultimately needs energy in the form of glycogen acquired from our diet. To climb well we need to be eating well.

Muscle fibre types

There is also a genetic predisposition towards either aerobic or anaerobic work. There are two types of (skeletal) muscle fibre, of which we all have a different proportion. We can train our bodies to adapt but a small difference in performance will remain.

Slow twitch muscle fibres are better at aerobic type work. It is often people with more of this type of muscle that perform better at long distance events like marathon running. You may be better adapted to long alpine style or mountain routes.

Fast twitch muscle fibres are more geared toward maximum strength and work in the anaerobic threshold. People with more of this type of fibre are better suited to sprinting. You may be better adapted to bouldering and short intense routes.

Overloading

If you go to a climbing wall and do the same session week after week your body will adapt to that routine but not improve beyond that. To train you must overload your body in one way or another so it can adapt further and gain in strength, stamina or anaerobic endurance.

Applying overload

Frequency – how often you train or climb.

Duration – length of time you train or climb for.

Intensity – the amount of routes you do in a given time.

Difficulty – the grade of route you climb in a session.

Quantity – the overall number of routes you do in a session.

Research shows that the greatest difference between elite and non-elite groups of climbers is the frequency of participation.

Frequency is perhaps the most important. As a rule of thumb the more often you climb the more the improvement you can expect. If you train just one day a week your ability may decrease. If you train two days a week you will likely be able to maintain your current ability. If you train three days a week you may well see an improvement. If you train four or more days a week you are likely to make marked improvements in your ability.

General vs specific

Consider how specific your training is to what you want to achieve. Whilst a weight-training regime might build individual muscles and circuit train-ing will work your general strengths, the majority of your training needs to be climbing-specific and targeted at your weaknesses. For example if you want to improve your arm strength then you could either go to a gym and pump iron (general training), or do steep overhanging routes on large holds (specific training).

Sequencing or periodisation

Whilst most climbers won't want to adopt a long term approach to training they may already be switching activities throughout the year which will help them in the long term. Many have a scattered approach and use the seasons to change to their preferred type of climbing. Changing between bouldering, ice climbing, sports climbing, traditional climbing on small outcrops and long mountain routes all in the space of a few months, weeks or even days. Whilst this approach might not be called 'sequence training' it will undoubtedly help you maintain your motivation for climbing.

Sequencing training

Each phase can last from 4 to 8 weeks, although with climbing an emphasis should be placed on strength, as this will help increase the ability in anaerobic and aerobic endurance. The training phases are: (1) Rest and recovery (2) Strength (3) Anaerobic (4) Aerobic (5) Peak performance phase (6) Repeat.

The peak performance phase is when you are approaching your physical and mental peak. Training at that time should be very specific, you should be training on and as near as possible to your dream goal. If you want to on-sight a route then you need to be practising on-sight climbing. If you compete then you should practise under competition conditions (for example the number and grades of routes or boulder problems you would be expected to complete during the event).

Example of sequenced training – for a climber who wants to peak over the summer months for a variety of rock climbing, and spends the winter training indoors from October onwards.

Recovery phase	October	2 days a week	Very easy top roping and leading for an active recovery.
Strength building phase	November – December	3 days a week	Bouldering to develop finger, arm, shoulder and core strength. Strength work in gym.
Anaerobic endurance	January – February	3 days a week	Interval training on hard routes. Long boulder problems. Circuit training/anaerobic gym work.
Aerobic endurance	March – April	3 days a week	Lots of easy route and boulder problems. Aerobic gym work (running, cycling, etc.)
Peak performance phase	April – May	3 days a week	1 day a week concentrating on each of the phases. Outdoor climbing specific to aims and goals.

See Training: Strength chapter for example exercises.

See Training: Endurance chapter for example exercises.

See Training: Fitness chapter for example exercises.

Training: Strength

To climb well you gonna need some of these, muscles!

Strength is the foundation of your training. Increases in strength make each move feel easier and that has a direct effect on both anaerobic and aerobic endurance. As the moves become easier, the level at which the pump occurs also rises. So, if you are only ever going to take the time to train one thing it should be strength. There are five major types of strength training:

General strength – the overall strength of your muscular system.

Specific strength – the strength of those muscles specific to the type of climbing you are pursuing.

Maximum strength – the greatest force that you can apply with one muscular contraction.

Explosive strength – the ability to apply your muscles as fast as possible.

Strength endurance – your ability to carry on aerobically or anaerobically. Endurance is addressed in the next two chapters.

Warm up thoroughly before you start any workout and stop when you feel yourself getting tired and sloppy (when injuries are most likely to occur). If you experience pain stop immediately. Continuing to train injured muscles you are likely to compound the injury and delay your recovery.

GENERAL STRENGTH

How strong your whole body is may not influence your climbing all that much but it does have implications for your general well being. Climbers often suffer from muscle imbalances as most of their training is pulling down with the hands and pushing up with the feet. After years of climbing this can lead to poor posture as the muscles you train overpower those that normally work in opposition to them.

So do some general strength exercises that work the muscles that climbing doesn't. Instead of pulling exercises do pushing ones. Circuit training is a great all round strengthening and aerobic activity, or you might choose to cross train in a sport which develops different muscle groups.

SPECIFIC STRENGTH

There are many types of specific strength that can improve your climbing and numerous ways to train each. It is up to you to choose which regimes best fit your climbing style, lifestyle, ability and commitment to training. The principle areas you might concentrate on are: fingers; arms and shoulders; core body; legs and feet.

Fingers

Fingers are the smallest weakest link in climbing; at times we use them to support our entire weight, something that they were not designed to do. Given a little care and a progressive approach, even your fingers can be trained to support your entire weight. It is very easy for our muscles to develop quicker than the connective tissue (ligaments, tendons and pulleys) that make up the internal workings of our fingers. So when starting out your fingers may be prone to injury.

Bouldering for finger strength – an ideal way to start developing your finger strength, along with good technique. At first this may be on vertical walls, but as you develop you need to move onto steeper ground. However if you move onto ground that is too steep too soon, you will stop working the fingers and start working the arms and shoulders, as you have to use bigger and bigger holds.

Start on a vertical wall climbing problems 6 to 8 moves long with small holds that come to either the first or second joint on your fingers. To be overloading your muscle you should be on routes that are just within the limit of your ability. If a move is too hard, start by making it easier by using bigger footholds then add overload by choosing progressively smaller footholds. The smaller the footholds you use the more weight comes onto the finger and the more body tension you will need to make the hold as good as possible. Complete about 8 routes with a three-minute rest between each. After the finger exercises you can move onto the arms and shoulders.

As you gain finger strength you will need to start upping the ante to keep on overloading your fingers. Choose smaller handholds and start thinking of moving onto a steeper wall, somewhere between 15 to 30 degrees overhanging, where you are still able to use small fingery holds. Again use bigger foot holds at first, eventually using the tiniest features.

Systems training – A name for another training method which isolates finger strength. Maintaining basic static positions on a wall with an overhanging angle of between 15 and 30 degrees. Many successful climbers who took training seriously like Wolfgang Güllich, Malcolm Smith and Ben Moon have used and developed this method. A 'Moon board' can be set up to help replicate moves and system training exercises, although similar moves can be mocked up on any climbing wall with a little imagination.

There are two variables in the systems training method. The first is what type of grip you use to grasp the hold, the second is the orientation in which you grab the hold. By working through each one you get a sixteen exercise permutation.

A Moon board, designed for systems training, similar to the setup in the famous UK training den the 'School Room'.

Grip position	Arm position
Full crimp	Downpull
Half crimp	Under cling
Open hand	Side pull
Pinch	Reverse side pull/back hand

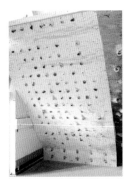

Each exercise comprises of holding a position with your left and right hand twice, and holding the position statically for 6 seconds, before changing hands. Have a 3 minute rest between sets, and try to work through all 16 permutation of the exercise. There should be no Egyptians, drop knees or other technical moves to take the weight off your hands, as you are deliberately trying to make the position as strenuous as possible. There are some a great example videos on the Moonclimbing website.

Finger boards – a simple tool for finger training. This is a simple selection of hand holds often placed above a door to help you train at home after work. Sometimes life simply gets in the way of going to the wall. They take up little space and are inexpensive compared to a home built wall.

The Fender Board by Beacon Climbing has a good selection of hold types.

Dan Varian, designer of the Beastmaker finger board, recommends training groups of fingers in this way on a finger board.

To gain strength on a finger board, warm up with a run and then a low number of pull ups on large holds on the board. Use the front three (index, middle and ring fingers) and back three (middle, ring and little fingers) grips on a variety of holds starting with large holds. Either just hang the holds or do up to four pull ups, before resting and moving onto smaller holds. If you can hold your weight with three fingers then you can advance onto adjacent pairs of fingers. Remember a tweak or slight pain is your body's way of warning you about injury; better to back off than injure yourself.

Arms and shoulders

The next weakest link in the climbing machine. You can move on to training your arms after your finger training session by using bigger holds and steeper terrain to isolate the arms and shoulders.

Bouldering for arm and shoulder strength – either as a stand alone session (after a thorough warm up) or continuing on from working on your finger strength session. Work on steep problems with big holds. Concentrate on making any movement slow and holding static shapes. The aim isn't to train power, so pull in a slow and controlled way, feeling the strain through the whole movement and lower yourself slowly in the same way.

Climb up to eight problems with a 3 minute rest between each problem. Add variety by doing some facing the wall and working the arms more than the shoulders. Then try twist-locking to work the shoulder more.

Straight on pulls work (A) the arms more, as you can see they are bent, whilst pulling upward with a twist-lock; (B) works the shoulders (as the arms are straight) and promotes better body position.

A Bachar ladder at the Indy climbing wall.

Footless arm and shoulder exercises – for some, simply bouldering on a steep wall will not overload your arms and shoulders. Take your feet off the wall to increase the load! Concentrate on slow controlled movement and holding static positions between movements.

Bachar ladder – climb the ladder hand over hand without your feet, using the lower hand to help push yourself up to a lock off and then reach the following rung. At first go up 6 rungs per set with a 3 minute rest between each set. Try for up to 6 sets.

Large campus board rungs – as for a Bachar ladder but on the large rungs of a campus board. Move as statically as possible. To develop it further use alternate rungs.

Pull up bars – simple to use and easy to install in a door frame. The key to training with a pull up bar is variety, alternating your grip from over hand, under hand, wide and narrow. Make your pull-ups slow and the descent controlled for maximum strength benefit. To start with try 6 pull ups a minute, every minute start on another 6 pull ups (continue for 4 sets or 4 minutes).

Typewriter – use a wide grip and pull up halfway, move your body across to the left keeping your shoulders at the same height parallel to the bar then back to the right. Repeat three times and rest for three minutes (continue for 4 sets).

Deep lock-offs – grab the bar with palms facing away from you (overhand grip) and pull up to the point where your chin touches the bar. Keeping your elbows low, try to push the bar towards your stomach as if trying to mantelshelf the bar. This will work the triceps as well as biceps.

Assisted one armers – a one arm pull up with a bungy aiding the movement or your other hand giving just enough support by pulling on some cord hanging down from the bar.

Unassisted one armers and locks – if you can do a one arm pull up unassisted well done! If you can't, try holding a 90˚ lock for three seconds. Rest for 3 minutes and then repeat again 6 times.

Weighted pull – if your body weight isn't enough resistance then hang some weights off a waist belt or harness. Start light and through trial and error build it up so that you begin to fail after 4 sets.

(A) basic pull ups off of pinches. (B) position to hold for a one-arm lock-off (try to maintain a 90° angle at your elbow).

(C) typewriter pull up, left to right and back again, maintaining a lock-off position.

Assisted one-arm pull up with (D) a chair and (E) a cord gripped low in the other hand.

Core body

Body tension and core strength are key ingredients to climbing well on all types of rock. On steeper terrain it helps you keep your feet on footholds and transfer power from the hands to the feet and vice versa.

Core strength is slow to develop through climbing alone, so specific core strength training is often useful. Pilates or yoga can be a great starting place for many (and both are also good for flexibility, balance and injury prevention).

Core strength is not the six pack or flat stomach of abdominal muscles, but a set of muscles hidden deep within pelvis, lower abdomen, back and hips. These muscles help stabilise the lower back and prevent back injuries. They are often overlooked for their more aesthetic surface muscles. With underdeveloped core strength and overdeveloped surface muscles you may be more prone to injury.

Core strength exercises at home – lie on your back and do some pelvic floor exercises. In men it is best described as trying to use your muscles to lift your testicles slightly. You should feel this in your lower abdomen, a muscle like a corset round the hips and lower back. At first hold for ten seconds and then work up until you can hold it for a minute. This takes practice to hold it for a minute, as you need to maintain tension in the lower abdomen but allow movement of the diaphragm to breathe. If you do not allow the diaphragm to move you start to engage other muscles, not isolating the correct muscle group.

Lie on your back and raise your feet 20–30 cm off the ground. Hold them there as static as you can for 10 seconds, then keeping them the same distance off the ground move your legs apart. Hold for another 10 seconds then move feet back together. As you develop more strength, repeat the exercise and see how long you can keep your feet off the ground.

Lying on your back again, raise your feet up on a sofa, then pushing your pelvis forward, straighten your back. Work up to holding the position for one minute.

Place your shoulder blades just onto a sofa, and walk your feet out until there is a 90°angle in the knees. Push your pelvis up to keep your hips in line. Work up to holding this position for at least a minute.

Get into a press up position but resting your elbows on the edge of your sofa and make your body into a straight board; work on holding this position for a minute.

These exercises will help to start to develop the core muscle group. They are good for beginners and intermediates, as they require less overall strength.

A selection of basic Pilates exercises. Most of these can be done at home with the sofa, no need for a Swiss ball (but they are good).

Core strength exercises on a pull up bar – more advanced exercises can be done on a pull up bar. Hang on the bar and slowly lift your knees to a sitting position and hold them there for 10 to 30 seconds before lowering back down slowly. At first you will only be able to do a few of these at a time.

An advancement on this exercise is to hang on bar and raise legs keeping them straight in a pike position and holding that position for 10 to 30 seconds, before lowering them slowly.

The most advanced exercise is a front lever, essentially a pull up where you keep your arms straight, and try and push the bar to your waist. This requires not only core strength, but massive amounts of body tension and shoulder strength.

Using a pull up bar to work on core muscles.
(A) Raising knees to chest.
(B) Performing a pike position.
(C) Holding the body as horizontal as possible, known as a front lever if you can get truly horizontal.

Core strength exercises at the wall – on an overhanging wall, reach up and hang off a jug. Now use your stomach muscles to lift your feet up to the side and place them on a hold. Attempt to do this as statically as possible, don't swing. To develop this try and reach a hold further and further to the side, or higher.

Using a steep bouldering wall to develop body tension. (Left) Pulling feet onto hold statically. (Right) Up ending the Plank.

Once you have placed your foot on the hold try and make your entire body as stiff as possible. Imagine a wooden plank that is linked between your hand and foot. When you have worked up the required strength, try hand traversing around, pivoting around your foot, as if you were trying to flip the plank over.

Another good exercise is to jump onto a steep wall and grab two holds. Try to imagine and hold a flamboyant body position in freeze frame that a photograph might capture the instant you latch the hold, before you swing. Try a different position, or have a game of who can hold the most outrageous position.

Legs and feet

Often overlooked because we use them all the time to stand on. There are several weak links in our legs that can become exhausted, resulting in 'disco', 'Elvis' or 'sewing machine' leg (involuntary twitching). This is often brought about through fear and bad technique. It stems from the muscles in the calf and feet becoming exhausted.

Leg and foot exercises – In order to isolate the weaker leg muscles, ignore good climbing technique and stand on your toes facing the wall applying maximum leverage through the calf and toes.

Climb steep slabs with little help from your hands. Concentrate on keeping the toes locked by trying to press an imaginary button under your big toe, engaging all your toes. Keep your ankle at 90° and do a few problems during your warm up like this to start developing foot strength worthy of a ballerina.

At home you can also work on this by balancing on the tips of your toes on a step and holding the position. Then rise up onto the tips of your toes, lower and repeat.

MAXIMUM STRENGTH

To become as strong as possible we need to apply an overloading factor beyond our own body weight. Performing some of the earlier strength exercises with a weight belt to get the required resistance to reach failure somewhere between 3 and 6 repetitions during each set.

There are two ways to become stronger, to grow more muscle fibres or to use more of your available muscle fibres with every effort. Strength training with mid loads (60% maximum) at low repetitions (3 – 10) and few sets (3 – 4) with short rests (1 minute or super sets of related exercises) will produce muscle growth (you should normally find yourself working hard enough so that you are unable to complete another set). Whereas training at very high loads (80% of the muscle's maximum) with very few repetitions (1 – 6) and longer rests between (15 minutes) will begin to increase your ability to recruit more fibres. It's understandably this 'recruitment training' which is of interest to top climbers as you can make gains in strength without gaining weight in muscle.

Recruitment training

To benefit from this type of training and to avoid injury you will need to be climbing at a level that will allow you to push yourself beyond the norm and have the strength within the connective tissue of your body to withstand the overloading that this type of training puts on the fingers, arms and shoulders. Typically you will be bouldering at a high level already (at least V4).

All these exercises require a thorough warm up, as well as a good warm down after the exercise.

The aim is to increase the number of muscle fibres used when trying to climb at 100% of our ability by resetting our muscles' 'safety valve'. This 'safety valve' is the feedback response to the Golgi tendon organ, the muscle's strain gauge that sends messages to the brain telling it that we are overexerting ourselves and likely to injure muscles, tendons or ligaments. Do a maximum of two recruitment sessions a week and allow between two or three days recovery.

> **Recruitment bouldering** – Move away from static movement and start using your power to help increase the loads to beyond what you can hold statically. The bouldering needs to be right at your limit or, at first, beyond it. Use short problems between 3 and 6 moves long. Allow 5 minutes rest between attempts. If you start feeling tired, weak or messy stop before you injure yourself.

Recruitment finger boards – Use a finger board to hold a finger position statically for around 6 seconds (full crimp, half crimp, pinch, etc.). You should be near failure when hanging the position, so you will either have to add weight with a weight belt (or reduce hold size) or reduce your weight by having some bungee cord attaching the fingerboard to your harness (or simpler, by placing your feet on a chair a couple of feet in front of you). Work through each hand position with the aim of only being able to hold one hang in each before having a five to ten minute rest before performing another position.

Recruitment campus boards – There are two exercises you can do. The first is touches – hang a rung with both hands and then reach up to touch a higher rung, before dropping back down and holding the starting position. Repeat 3 times for each hand. Allow a 5 to 10 minute rest between sets. Use full, half and open handed crimps.

The second exercise is a series of double dynos starting from the first rung and going up two, and then quickly dropping down one rung; as soon as you hit the lower rung, explode back up another two rungs. So the sequence is 1 to 3 to 2 to 4 to 3 to 5 to 4 to 6. Try for at least 3 sets with a 10 minute rest between each set.

EXPLOSIVE STRENGTH (POWER)

As your climbing gets harder the distance between holds increases and it becomes necessary to power through the moves, either lunging for or, in extreme circumstances, jumping for a hold. Technique for lunges and dynos is covered in the earlier chapter Advanced Technique & Bouldering. Using and controlling your explosive strength is a skill that can take years to develop. You need explosive power, coordination and contact finger strength.

You will be climbing English 6a or V4 with the goal of bouldering even harder before you have developed the musculoskeletal strength to benefit from this type of training (which can easily lead to injury).

Typically an explosive move is proceeded by a short drop or bounce to stretch the muscles, storing energy in the elasticity of the tendon and muscle to add to the rapid contraction of muscles. Muscles, tendons and ligaments are going to be pushed to their limit so they need to be warmed up and ready.

Explosive power must be used quickly, dropping into a stretch phase and instantly powering out of it. Any pause or repeated bouncing will only loose stored elastic energy.

Explosive power exercise – Try out three lunges. First pull onto a wall and without dipping down use your power to jump as far as possible. Next, dip down (bending your whole body away from your target) quickly and power up out of the dip to jump as far and fast as possible. Finally, dip down and hold the dip for 5 seconds before launching upwards.

You should have reached further with the quick dip and jump, as the elastic energy stored as you dip helps drive you up. Holding the dip allows your muscles to react to the stretch, releasing some of the tension which results in less recoil.

Explosive hand and arm training – On a campus board choose a size of rung or hold that you can happily hang with both hands and double dyno up two rungs, hang that rung momentarily, before dropping down one rung. As soon as you have got your hands on that rung, start resisting the downward force, this will store up elastic energy, and power up again two rungs. In short, double dyno rung 1 to 3 to 2 to 4 to 3 to 5. Start with two or three reps, have a 5 minute rest between sets.

As you develop tendon and finger strength you may find yourself able to use smaller holds, or dyno to further rungs.

Explosive leg training – Most climbers have a enough explosive strength in their legs, and the majority will not need to work on this exercise. Stand on a block between 30cm and 50cm high, and jump off; as you land instantly try and jump up as high as possible.

Explosive moves – The trick now is to get the timing of the drive from the legs to work in time with the drive from the upper body, which just takes practice. On a steep wall, set up for a lunge or jump to a good hold, then drop down and drive as hard as possible with arms and legs.

The last part of controlling explosive strength is landing; it is all well and good being able to jump a long way, but you'll need to hang the hold at the end. To start with aim for large holds with either one or both hands, to limit the possibility of injury. Eventually the combination of good timing, judging distance and core body tension will make it possible to land small holds a long way away.

Contact finger strength exercise – Using a campus board or over-hanging wall, stand on the ground and get hold of either a suitable sized rung or two holds. Jump up and try and grasp a hold above. At first you may over or under shoot the target hold; eventually you should get the right length of jump, with your hand reaching the 'dead point', or apex of the jump, as you reach the hold.

As you start to more constantly reach the hold, concentrate on what happens to your body after you have reached the hold. To start with see what happens if you totally relax your body when you reach the hold. Then try and engage your core strength to point one or both toes as close to the wall as possible.

What you should notice is that when you engage your core you won't swing out from the wall as much, in essence you are almost trying to hold your body in a freeze frame at the moment you arrive at the hold.

Training: Endurance

(Above) Pumped out
of your tiny mind, you
are seconds away from
failure, but inches from
the finishing holds.

Often we start to call on our anaerobic endurance when we are already being pushed to the limit. As soon as you start to feel the pump building the clock is ticking (failure is not far away). Whilst it is impossible to rid our bodies of the need to work anaerobically, the body can be conditioned to fight it. You might:

Develop a higher aerobic threshold, raising the level of the onset of blood lactate accumulation (OBLA).

Increase your strength so the moves are easier.

Develop a greater awareness of how hard and long you can keep going through the pump so that you can choose your rests wisely.

Condition your muscles to work better during anaerobic activity.

The first two choices keep us out of the red zone, take a look at the previous section on Strength or the next section on Fitness to help with this. The third choice comes down to learning just when you have actually reached failure, as opposed to just feeling like you are failing. Training anaerobic endurance will help with this as you try to push yourself that extra 10% more than you thought possible. Conditioning your muscles to anaerobic endurance involves training in our anaerobic zone, helping us to develop ways in which to cope and recover better from higher and higher levels of blood lactate accumulation.

This means working on routes and longer boulder problems that test you to the limit, resting for approximately twice the time it takes to complete the exercise. Ideally the activity should last for somewhere between one and two minutes, constantly above the aerobic threshold. A good starting point is a sustained route, rather than one with just one hard move, that is one grade below your on-sight limit, preferably a route that you know so failure will be through fatigue rather than using a wrong sequence of moves. Increase the overload as you improve. If you started by making six laps of a route with twice the length of time to recover then you can either increase number of laps, the grade of route or reduce the recovery time.

Anaerobic training – Find a route you know well, that is one grade below your on-sight limit. Start by making up to 6 laps of the route, with twice as much recovery time as it takes to climb the route. Each session apply a little more overload, by increasing the grade of the route, the number of reps or reduce the time you allow for recovery.

Bouldering for anaerobic endurance (lapping routes) – Use a long sustain traverse or long problems between 12 and 20 moves long. Rest for twice the time you were climbing for, and make six laps of the route.

Bouldering is one of my favourite ways to increase anaerobic endurance, by seeing how many problems I can link by climbing up one and down another.

Bouldering for anaerobic endurance (linking problems) – Every time you go to the wall increase the number of times you complete a set link-up of problems, up one and down another and so on. Overload can be increased by adding on a harder problem at the start, or by reducing the rest. This becomes strangely addictive, as you try to add more and more problems over the weeks to your 'big link!'

Bouldering for anaerobic endurance (stick method) – Have a friend with a stick to point at the next hold you can use – keep this going for a set period of time or number of moves, then swap over whilst you rest. This can add more creative and varied practice to your movement. Aim to start off with at least 20 moves or 3 minutes on the wall. To add overload up the time or the number of moves.

Fingerboard interval training – On a fingerboard or pull up bar do three to six pull ups every minute (dependent on your fitness), trying to complete a minimum of ten repetitions to a maximum of twenty. Use a stopwatch or clock with a second hand. After each set of pull ups rest for the remainder of the minute before starting the next set on the next minute. You can change the width of your grip or the holds you use.

Fingerboard pyramid training – Hang a position for a set time before resting for five seconds and hanging the same position for a progressively longer time – working up in increments.

4 second hang – 5 second rest

6 seconds hang – 5 second rest

8 seconds hang – 5 second rest

10 seconds hang – 5 second rest

8 seconds hang – 5 second rest

6 seconds hang – 5 second rest

4 seconds hang – 5 second rest

1 minute rest

Repeat this pyramid 10 times. Once this becomes easier reduce the length of the rests or reduce the size of the holds.

Pete Robins working strength at the Mill.

Fingerboard pyramid training 2 – With an interval of one minute do one pull up and rest for the remainder of the minute, then two pull ups and rest for the remainder of the minute, continue to do 3, 4, 5, 6, 7, 8, 9, 10, 9, 8, 7, 6, 5, 4, 3, 2, 1. At first you may only reach 6 or so pull ups, wherever you reach failure start to decrease the reps on each interval. The full exercise will take twenty minutes and you will have completed 100 pull ups by the end of the session.

Fingerboard repeaters – Hold a grip for 7 seconds and rest for three. Repeat this for a minute (6 reps) then take a minute rest. Try to get to 10 sets of 6 reps, beyond which you can reduce the minutes rest to add overload.

You can make these hangs harder by alternating the grip, either reduce the size of hold, or reduce the number or change the configuration of fingers. Using what is dubbed the front three (Index, middle, ring fingers) or back three hang (middle, ring, little fingers).

Overload can be increased by going through the different sets of two finger holds, and finally monos. One finger holds are for experts only, as they are highly likely to result in finger injury!

General anaerobic endurance

In addition to specific anaerobic training, general anaerobic training will help too. Such as some high intensity circuit training either using resistance exercises in the gym, working on a high number of reps and lower resistance, or doing other forms of circuit training like press ups, sit ups, squat thrusts, etc. Use a set time on each activity or work station before moving on.

Anaerobic gym exercises – After warming up work flat out for 3 to 5 minutes perhaps on exercise machines like versa climbers or rowing machines. Your muscles should feel like they are burning through lactic acid build up. Have a rest for the same time or less than the time spent exercising. Start with 6 sets of the activity and either decrease the resting period or increase the number of sets.

Training: Fitness

You don't have train indoors; long easy routes outside can help as well. Savage Sunbird, Rhoscolyn.

After strength training, aerobic exercise is the next best way to improve all areas of your climbing, because aerobic fitness puts off the onset of blood lactate accumulation (OBLA) and also is the means by which you recover from the pump. Your aerobic fitness improves by promoting capillary growth and also developing efficiency in your heart and lungs, both of which increase the flow of oxygenated blood to the muscles (your VO_2 max). Time spent climbing within your aerobic threshold will lead to capillary growth where it's needed and your heart and lungs can be exercised by any general aerobic work.

Aerobic exercise will be at a level where you don't start to feel pumped, this is often at an easier level then most people think. There isn't a cut off point were we stop working aerobically and switch entirely to anaerobic work. Instead the onset of blood lactate accumulation leads progressively to parts of the muscle switching to anaerobic activity.

Work on your aerobic endurance by climbing lots of easy routes, in order to promote capillary growth in the climbing muscles. You will also need to work on your general fitness by running, taking brisk walks, swimming, cycling etc. to develop your heart and lungs to supply the extra oxygen required. Any type of activity is good as long as we keep it within our aerobic threshold and it lasts for at least 20 minutes but preferably up to 1 hour. You need to work at a leisurely pace and increase either the time you are training for, the distance covered or the time in which you are covering a set distance.

Log your sessions – improvements can be hard to keep track of. You can measure your VO_2 max with this simple test at the beginning of your training and after several weeks revisit the test and see how you have improved.

Working out your VO_2 max (the Balke test) – Use a 400m track, GPS watch or treadmill to find the maximum distance you can run on the flat in 15 minutes.

$$\frac{(\text{Total distance covered} \div 15) - 133}{0.172} + 33.3 = VO_2 \text{ max}$$

Climbing-specific fitness

Extend your warm-up by climbing easy routes and adding the crucial overload by increasing the length (time of training session and number of routes), frequency (number of sessions a week), intensity (number of routes per hour) or difficulty (grade of routes climbed aerobically).

Aerobic capillary exercise – In order to make your aerobic workout something other than a constant climbing up and down routes, it is good to set yourself a series of technique exercises, breaking down the monotony of climbing lots of easy routes.

Face left

Face right

Face sideways (left and right pivoting between the two)

Silently

Quickly

Slowly

As fast as possible

Fluidly

Aggressively

Hands below shoulders

Rule of opposites

Developing as many hands-off rests as possible

Aerobic training tips

If you start to feel pumped the route is too hard.

Keep the effort going for as long as possible (at least a hour).

Focus on technique to maintain concentration.

Apply overload through length of session, number of routes in session, frequency of sessions or careful increase in difficulty.

Cross training

Finding time for fitness training in your week can be hard. Other sports can provide a diverting way to stay active in a way which fits your lifestyle. You need to be looking for an activity that you can sustain at a moderate pace for half an hour but preferably longer, and be able to make the effort to do it twice a week. Many of us won't have broken a sweat since we left school but that's what you should be aiming for. As well as aerobic fitness, this type of exercise will help you to lose weight and feel healthier.

Mountain biking and cycling

A massive and growing sport in UK, during the summer months a great way to get your aerobic exercise outdoors. Most rides take at least half an hour and it uses the body's biggest muscle group, the legs, bum and lower back. Cycling to and from work can be a great way to rack up exercise time. In the winter it can be hard to keep the motivation up to go cycling when it is blowing an icy north wind driving sleet into your face.

Running

Perhaps the easiest aerobic exercise to get into, all you need is a pair of trainers. Easily slotted into your routine by running after work and a half hour run can be made in lulls between your favourite television programs, so instead of sitting and watching telly for the hell of it, put your trainers on and get your heart rate up.

Swimming

Great aerobic exercise that puts very little strain or impact on the joints, unlike running. It also exercises the upper body making a great all round conditioning exercise that may also help capillary development in the muscles of the arms, shoulders and upper body.

Mountaineering/scrambling/walking

As climbers many of us have walked uphill to crags and/or scrambled back down again. It's very good aerobic conditioning sport as during the course of a day out in the mountains you can call on all major muscle groups used in climbing. Walking can be a good back-up plan for when you arrive somewhere to climb only to find the cliff wet.

Kayaking

Canoe sport is great for the core and upper body; including whitewater, placid water racing, canoe polo, sea or surf kayaking. As an adventure sport whitewater paddling often appeals to climbers. River paddling in the UK often requires rain, so at times it is possible to kayak when it is not possible to climb. Equipment can be expensive and it may help to get some coaching to participate safely and enjoyably. Try it out at a local canoe club.

Surfing

Good upper body exercise, surfing also develops balance. It's a lot more fun than swimming endless lengths of a pool. Whilst it may take years to master, something simpler like body boarding is easy to enjoy and will appeal to the adventurous. In places like Pembroke and Cornwall it is possible to climb during the day and surf during the late afternoon/early evening.

Join a gym

A gym close to your home or work can make finding time to exercise easier. Variation in your training will help keep the motivation up and be better for your general fitness. Most gyms are equipped with treadmills, cross trainers, cycle machines and such like as well as holding regular circuit training classes and even swimming pools and squash courts.

Training: The Young Climber

This section is adapted from work by Dr Istvan Balyi (a world leader on the subject of long term athlete development)

Some sports like gymnastics require early specialisation before the age of 8 to reach the peak of personal performance. Others, like climbing, are late specialisation sports where it can be detrimental to train too hard too early.

There are phases in a youngster's growth where specific skills can be trained at an augmented rate. Chronological age is not as good an indicator as biological age, which is determined by growth rate. Of particular importance is the adolescent growth spurt (PHV or peak height velocity).

Variation between male and female onset of the adolescent growth spurt. Keep an eye out for this by measuring height monthly and comparing it from year to year.

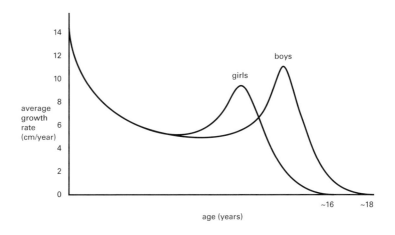

There are optimum times to change the phases of long term training, ages when the body can more easily adapt and develop skills and strengths.

FUNdamentals – (male 6–9, female 5–8 years)

Exercise at this stage should be structured but fun with the emphasis on developing basic movement (agility, balance and coordination, the ABCs). For general fitness, participation in a range of sports is best. At the end of this phase is a period when you can start to develop speed. Any strength exercises should use only the child's own body weight or a medicine ball.

Learning to train – (male 9–12, female 8–11 years)

During this stage young climbers should learn the basic movement skills of climbing and other sports. It coincides with a child's heightened development of motor coordination. Introduce a variety of climbing styles like slabs, walls, corners, arêtes etc. Learning the very basics of why and how to train general fitness like flexibility, speed, warming up and warming down. Any strength exercises should use the child's own body weight or a medicine ball.

Training to train – (male 12–16, female 11–15 years)

Further gains can be made in general physical ability and training aerobic capacity can begin. Ideally aerobic training should wait until after the onset of PHV when rapid growth of the body allows increased improvement to aerobic capacity. More emphasis on how to stretch is useful (as the bones and ligaments are growing rapidly), as well as the basics of nutrition and mental preparation.

Training to perform – (male 16–18, female 15–17 years)

Continued importance on physical conditioning with the focus on developing general strength using free weights. The skills and tactics of advanced climbing should be introduced, such as preparation, mental coping skills, reading routes, onsighting and redpointing.

Training to win – (male 18+, female 17+ years)

Time to specialise and train specifically in one or more styles of climbing and to pursue the dream goals.

Some people can get very competitive about climbing, a sense of competition among peers can be good motivation but climbing is really all about enjoyment. After all many people starting off climbing at a young age stay active for life. Climbing is a sport for life!

Turn training into play, rather than for improvement at the cost of pleasure. Over-training and pushy coaches and parents often leads to disillusionment and burn-out in young climbers who give up the sport.

long term development risks

How the bones in our hands and feet develop. The soft cartilaginous tissue can deform if we train our fingers too hard before they have finished growing, or jam young feet into over-tight shoes.

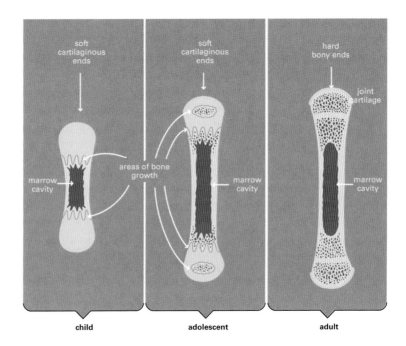

soft cartilaginous ends

soft cartilaginous ends

hard bony ends

joint cartilage

areas of bone growth

marrow cavity

marrow cavity

marrow cavity

child   **adolescent**   **adult**

Climbing can have a detrimental effect on an under-developed body which can have long lasting medical repercussions.

Deformation of the fingers is often preceded by finger pain, young climbers need to be aware of this and take precautions to avoid over-stressing their joints.

Fingers are one of the most at risk parts of the body in young climbers. Our skeleton doesn't fully mature until we reach 20. During puberty the weight and muscle gained following the growth spurt can cause a series of micro traumas (particularly in males). Early training has led in some cases to permanent finger deformity in the 3rd or 4th fingers. The close association between testosterone and muscle growth often leads to individual males 'outgrowing their own strength' around their growth spurt. Muscles develop strength more rapidly than the ligaments, bones and tendons. General strength can be developed during this period, and it is specifically the fingers that are at risk from climbing training. Avoid steep, powerful and fingery bouldering, and campus and finger board training is a strict no-no. Instead look more at lead climbing and psychological skill development to avoid injury and possible lay-off from climbing.

We all know that rock shoes need to be tight and that children's feet grow rapidly but studies show that if we wear unnaturally shaped or too tight rock shoes then there is a risk of foot injury or deformity.

Training tips for young people –

Under 16s should not undertake intensive finger strength training – avoid high intensity bouldering.

A force which would tear and adult's ligament will inflict far greater damage on a youngster. Parts of the fingers are 2 to 5 times weaker than the surrounding tissue.

The final growth spurt at the end of puberty can lead to young climbers 'out growing their strength'.

Up to 12 years old children have a limited capacity to adapt specifically to climbing but have a greater ability to develop general motor skills. So under twelves benefit most from very varied climbing practice (corners, grooves, slabs, arêtes, etc.)

Avoid wearing excessively tight rock shoes before the age of 15.

It's a good time to learn about the importance of a well balanced diet and the timing of intake.

There is limited evidence that early rock climbing can lead to back problems in later life!

The age at which climbers should specialise in climbing is unknown.

Training programmes should be designed by experienced people who carefully monitor a child's development in relation to their biological age.

Nutrition

This chapter could be written in two words, 'eat sensibly'. In a modern world of 'organic' this and 'super food' that we are losing sight of our evolutionary history. Humans are omnivorous; we evolved to eat both meat and vegetables, we didn't specialise. We ate whatever was available. Some people will be vegetarians but it is easier to have a balanced diet if you eat meat and unless you are careful to ensure enough protein in your diet you may never reach your maximum physical potential. For our climbing we need energy to perform and nutrients to rebuild muscles afterwards.

Sitting here reading this book your body is burning energy obtained from what you have eaten. Our fuel is typically carbohydrate, but we also need a whole host of nutrients to maintain a healthy body.

Proteins are needed for growth and the repair of muscles and body tissue.

Fats are a source of energy and are important to some vitamins that are only soluble in fat.

Carbohydrates are the main energy source that our bodies use.

Minerals are inorganic elements (iron, calcium, phosphorous, etc.) that are needed in small amounts as the building blocks of our bodily systems.

Vitamins are water or fat-soluble compounds that are needed in the chemical processes within our bodies.

Water makes up 60% of our body and carries nutrients around.

Roughage is the indigestible fibre in our diet which
helps to maintain a healthy digestive track.

All of the above will be present in a normal healthy fresh meat and veg-etable diet. Processed food will contain fewer useful nutrients. The modern world has found ways to get more and more 'food' out of less and less raw produce, e.g. Turkey Wotsits. Whilst ready meals and convenience food are part of modern lifestyle the value of taking time to prepare your own 'real' food shouldn't be underestimated. Where do you get these key nutrients?

Protein – fish, poultry, meat, dairy

Fats – meat, fish, dairy, vegetable, nut and seed oils.

Carbohydrates – pasta, rice, bread, oats, fruit,
sugar, potatoes and other root vegetables.

Vitamins and minerals – meat, fish, poul-try, colourful vegetables, salads, fruit.

Water – best drunk from a mountain stream.

Roughage – plant fibre from oats, cereal, fruit and some vegetables.

Most of what you need will come from a totally traditional diet of eating nice fresh vegetables, fruit, meat, fish, poultry and bread. It isn't rocket science, just common sense. A balanced diet requires all these nutrients to maintain a healthy equilibrium.

Our energy requirement is like a bank account, if we pay in too much we get a large balance, storing the excess as fat. If we don't deposit enough energy into our bank we start to eat away at our reserves of fat and poten-tially heading for malnutrition, starting to break down muscles and bone for energy. Under-fed you will run out of energy to climb.

The ideal is to maintain a net zero economy, for this you need to know two things, your basic energy requirement when you aren't training and what extra energy you need for training. You need to have enough energy for effective climbing and to supply your body with enough fuel.

WARNING for coaches and parents – Offering reward for losing weight or punishment for gaining weight. Even what seems like a throw away comment will increase the likelihood of that person developing an eating disorder. An adult may be old enough to be relied on to make their own decisions to lose weight to improve performance but a child cannot. Weighing children at all is debatable given current research. Is their health worth it?

How much energy do you need?

At rest, working, climbing or training we use energy at different rates. If you are going to exercise today, eat more food to give you more energy. Do what feels right. There is no need to count the calories you consume unless you are competing at world championship level, in which case you should really seek the advice of a trained dietician.

How do you monitor your weight?

Is there any need to weigh yourself? You are after all into climbing for fun. Your clothes are a simple indication of weight gain or loss. Some people will look at their bodies excessively in the mirror with a critical eye (I am too fat, I am not thin enough, I have lost too much weight). Weighing yourself on the bathroom scales is simple enough, but changes in your weight are more likely to be affected by muscle gain than through the gaining or losing of fat.

A better but by no means flawless way to monitor your weight and body fat is to calculate your body mass index (BMI). Given your build, weight and height it can give a rough estimate of your body fat compared to some general population data. There are many BMI calculators online.

More accurate, but still only approximate, is to use a bioelectrical impedance analysis (BIA) machine, which you may find in your gym. The machine passes a current through you and (using your height, weight and other information) estimates your body composition and percentage of body fat.

When to eat?

Unfortunately eating is not like refuelling a car, food is not instantly usable as fuel. Eat a meal too soon before exercise and your body will struggle to digest the food; it will divert energy to your stomach to help with digestion, making it even less available for climbing.

When to eat for effective exercise

Large meals need to be eaten 3 to 4 hours before exercise.

Small meals need to be eaten 2 to 3 hours before exercise.

Light Snacks can be eaten 10 to 15 minutes before exercise.

Avoid skipping meals as your body needs time to replenish itself from your diet. Faced with a choice of either not eating before exercise or just eating some bananas, chocolate, flapjack or sweets, it is best to eat something.

Some foods are described as being high or low glycemic index (GI), which means that they have a greater or lesser effect at raising our blood sugar levels over time. A high GI food will more rapidly increase blood sugar levels but will create just a short peak before that level reduces. A low GI food will take longer to raise blood sugar levels but will sustain those levels for longer.

Before and during long day out climbing

In order to manage your energy levels for an entire day out we need start at breakfast, filling up with enough medium and low GI foods to last us as long as possible throughout the day. Again we need to eat a couple hours before we go out; this sometimes isn't possible, although knowing the average climber's 'Alpine' start it may not prove too difficult. Remember to concentrate on hydrating at breakfast.

You are also going to need to take some food with you, in the form of a packed lunch or a series of snacks. Some people will prefer the little bits of food and often approach to topping up their energy levels, whilst others will prefer to stop and have a packed lunch. Whatever your choice a whole day out climbing will require you to refuel and re-hydrate throughout the day, if you want to carry on climbing at the same level.

Before climbing a short intense route

If you're out climbing and you have warmed up and want to climb a hard intense route consider refuelling with a high energy drink, energy bar, chocolate or other food with a High GI rating, half hour or so before climbing. The energy you get will be short, but it might give you the edge you need.

Before an evening training

If you're at work, and you plan to train that evening think about what time you will get to the wall and eat three hours before you get there. A reasonable lunch or good sized afternoon snack will help give you the energy you need to train. Also consider making sure you are suitably hydrated by taking on fluid.

If you are eating a reasonable meal that is low GI then three hours before the training session is fine. If however you don't have three hours because you forgot then consider a smaller medium/high GI meal.

During exercise

Unless the activity is going to last over 90 minutes it will be unnecessary to replenish carbohydrates. If you are going to exercise for longer than 90 minutes then consider drinking an energy/sports/isotonic drink. It should have enough carbohydrate/sugar to keep you going and have some salt (sodium and potassium) content to fight off cramps.

During exercise we lose water through perspiration and exertion, so in order to replenish our hydration level we need to drink at least half a cup of water every twenty minutes. Adding flavour to water has been shown to encourage fluid uptake and prolong activity.

After exercise

After exercise your muscles will be depleted of their stored carbohydrates. By eating high GI foods and drink the blood sugar will rapidly increase and will be quickly absorbed into the muscles which will help aid the repairing and rebuilding of muscles, as well as replenishing our natural store of energy in our muscles. High energy drinks or food immediately after exercise will help you recover quicker.

Fluids

Replacing water is simple enough! Have you drunk enough of the right fluids? How we judge this is more guess work than science. Our urine is an indicator, clear = hydrated; bright yellow = dehydrated.

Bananas are a good source of potassium.

When we pass water (and when we sweat) we also excrete sodium, chloride and potassium among other things, all of which we need to replace in order to maintain our fluid balance. Sodium maintains blood pressure and helps nerve impulses, sodium bicarbonate helps to maintain normal acidity in our blood; chloride works with sodium for water balance, as well as electrolyte and stomach acid; and potassium helps nerve impulses and is involved in muscle function.

In extreme cases marathon/long distance runners have suffered from hyponatraemia, continually sweating, using electrolytes and drinking only water all the electrolytes are washed out of their bodies. It is very hard to over-hydrate unless you are running a marathon in very hot conditions.

On all but the hottest of days or longest climbing wall sessions, a sensible diet and drinking water will more than suffice. Isotonic 'sports drinks' are glucose and electrolyte solutions, which will help with more marathon efforts. Look for evidence on the label that the drink contains some of the electrolytes that you lose during exercise.

Hydration and salts

If you go on a climbing trip to a very hot area, then your body will take a period of time to adjust to the heat and reduce the amount you sweat. Until that point consider using isotonic drinks to replace the salts rather than just water alone.

Nutrition basics

Eat 2 to 4 hours before exercise

Stay hydrated

Avoid processed food

Try eating fresh foods

Replenish your energy supplies after exercise.

Nutritional supplements

Try to avoid the need to take supplements to your food, but sometimes the modern lifestyle gets in the way. Consult your doctor or dietician before taking dietary supplements.

Lifestyle is more important, don't think by taking supplement means you can disregard maintaining a healthy lifestyle.

Supplements are no replacement for healthy eating.

Large doses of single nutrients can be detrimental to your health.

Supplements as 'alternative' medical treatment may lead you to not seeking proper help.

The quality and content of supplements may vary.

Some dietary supplements impair health or cause death e.g. some weight loss pills.

Some of the more common supplements that are taken by active people are mentioned below. Some have effects of enhancing performance, others preventing injury or counteract dietary insufficiencies.

Vitamins and minerals

Other than suggesting that the majority of healthy eaters will get the majority of vitamins and minerals from their diet, there is very little else I'd like to add; full lists of vitamins and minerals and where we can source them in a normal diet, as well as their effect in the human body, can be found in dedicated nutrition texts or online.

One important element is calcium, which is involved in bone growth and strength, and also in muscular processes. The second is iron. If you are starting a training programme your body's reaction is often to increase red blood cell count which needs iron, so it might be important to increase foods high in iron if you are starting a training regime. You are unlikely to become anaemic through exercise, so don't rush out for the iron tablets.

Glucosamine

This is often taken by older people to alleviate the pain associated with arthritis. Active sports people take it to help repair any damage they might do to their joints through exercise. In particular, running can have a high impact on the knees, as can walking down steep hills from mountain cliffs. There is growing research that supports the glucosamine as aiding the joints.

Cod liver oil

Performance enhancing drugs are ethically questionable whether you are climbing for fun or competition.

Similar to glucosamine, cod liver oil is seen as a supplement to helps joints, but has also been shown to help the heart, bones, and brain, as well as nourish skin, hair and nails. It is also high in vitamins A & D.

Creatine

At present creatine has been shown to be safe and is not a banned substance under the World Anti Doping Agency. It's commonly used by athletes. Nevertheless, this information on creatine is not a recommendation.

Creatine is a performance enhancing substance, that occurs naturally in meats. However it is one of the more common sporting supplements, in the form of an artificially synthesised version that some athletes consume in order to improve their performance.

It has been shown to improve strength and endurance in a variety of test situations but is associated with increased body mass, through water retention in the muscles caused by the higher levels of creatine attracting more fluid inside every cell. It is therefore potentially disadvantageous for climbing.

A 5–7 gram dose four times a day for two days is enough creatine to significantly increase creatine levels in the muscles (doses may vary, dependent on source). Some research has shown that it becomes less effective if used in conjunction with caffeine, but I can't tell you how many cups of rich, dark, aromatic coffee it takes to make creatine supplements useless.

Carbohydrate supplements

Some people will take carbohydrate supplements to help them perform and train. Whilst on the one hand this is a simple way to ensure you have the correct energy level for training and recovery, it should be noted that they aren't an alternative to a healthy diet.

Where they might come in handy is if you are going to have an intensive training period, where you really push yourself physically. It is often in these periods of intensive training that athletes have reported over training or over-reaching, and performance has actually dropped. Research into this phenomenon has shown that a high carbohydrate diet can help to buffer an athlete from overtraining syndrome.

EATING DISORDERS & SPORT

In a sport where body image or body weight are important, people can often feel under pressure to be thin. It is important to spot eating disorders before they become problematic or even life threatening.

If you suspect someone has an eating disorder you should seek professional advice from a GP, doctor or specialist counsellor before confronting the individual with your opinion.

Typically young women suffer eating disorders, often when there is a major transition in their life (perhaps from school to college or university). There are many triggers and men and women of all ages can also suffer. In women anorexia can lead to what is referred to as the female athlete triad; where disordered eating leads to amenorrhea (the loss of the period for three months or more) and early onset osteoporosis (weakening of the bones).

WARNING signs of anorexia nervosa – People who suffer from anorexia nervosa are obsessed with controlling their eating. The reason for their obsession is the belief that by controlling their bodies they can control their lives. This obsession is often achieved through starvation and can have the following warning signs:

Dramatic weight loss.

Preoccupation with food, calories and weight.

Wearing baggy/layered clothing.

Relentless/excessive exercise.

Mood swings.

Avoiding food-related social activities.

WARNING signs of bulimia nervosa – People who suffer from Bulimia nervosa often go through cycles of bingeing and purging. As with anorexia, this behaviour is driven by a desire to regulate feelings.

The cycle begins with the eating of large amounts of food in a single sitting often to numb uncomfortable feelings, like anger or sadness. But it also creates physical discomfort and anxiety about weight gain. In an attempt to rid the body of this food a sufferer will vomit, use laxatives, have enemas or use diuretics, as well as using exercising, skipping meals and dieting, often inappropriately. The warning signs are:

Fluctuations in body weight.

Using diet pills, laxatives or diuretics.

Going to the bathroom after eating.

Signs of throwing up.

Depression.

Mood swings.

Low self esteem.

Damage to tooth enamel (appears clear).

Isolation, withdrawal and secretive behaviour.

WARNING signs of anorexia athletica – Anorexia athletica is a condition where people over-exercise because they believe this will control their bodies and give them a sense of power, control and self-respect. It isn't a clinically recognised diagnosis in the same way that anorexia nervosa or bulimia are, but compulsive exercising can have serious health consequences. Although not as well recognised or as dangerous as anorexia or bulimia, the warning signs are:

Exercising more than is good for our health.

Being fanatical about our weight and diet.

Taking time off work, school and relationships to exercise.

Focusing on the challenge exercise poses, and forgetting that it can be fun.

Believing that our self-worth depends on our physical performance.

Rarely being satisfied by what we achieve physically.

Saying that this exercise is okay because we are athletes, or insisting that the behaviour is healthy.

Index

A

ABC (anchors, belay, climber) 17
abrasion 43
abseiling 49, 50, 52
adolescent growth spurt 207
ADP (adenosine diphosphate) 181
aerobic respiration 181, 203, 204
alloy gate karabiners 144
anaerobic respiration 181
angles 20, 22
anorexia athletica 219
anorexia nervosa 218
anxiety 170, 171
arêtes, resting 95
arêtes, climbing 110
arm-bar 86
arousal 169, 171
ATP (adenosine triphosphate) 181

B

Bachar ladder 175, 189
back and footing 94, 96
back clipping 141
balance 65, 89
Balke test 204
belay devices 37
belaying 34
Ben Moon 187
BMC Participation Statement 8
body mass index 213
bolts 31, 32
bottom rope 34
bottom roping 16, 23
bouldering 52, 117, 184
bouldering mat 52
buddy system 37
bulimia nervosa 219

C

campus board 125, 189
cams 33, 147, 148
carbohydrate supplements 218
catastrophe effect 169
centre of gravity 70, 120
chalk bags 41
chicken wing 86
chimneys, resting 96
chimneys, climbing 111, 112

climb when ready 47
clip-drop training 174
clipping quickdraws 139–143
clip stick 152
clove hitch 25, 27
cod liver oil 217
Colin Kirkus 109
confidence 159
contact finger strength 124, 198
core strength 191, 192, 193
corkscrew rock-overs 102–104
cork traverse 74
corners 105
creatine 217
cupping 78

D

Dan Varian 188
dead-mans handle 51, 52
deadpoint 123
dead rope 34, 36
directional 19
disco leg 194
dogged 137
double ropes 155–158
drop knee 120
drop knees 187
dynamic moves 123
dynos 125, 126

E

eating disorders 218
edge protection 23, 24
edging, feet 68
Egyptians 120, 187
Elvis leg 194
equalised 19–22
equipment life 41–43
extenders 149–151

F

fall factor 48
fast twitch muscle fibres 183
fear of falling 174
finger boards 188
finger strength 186
fist-jams 85
flagging 89, 90
flash 136

focus 172, 173
foot-locks 121
Frankenjura 127
French free 137
French prussic 51
front lever 193
FUNdamentals 208

G

gate chatter 144
gear loops 38
gear placement 27
general vs specific (training) 183
glucosamine 217
goal setting 178, 179
gripper clipper 152
ground up 136
guidebooks 132

H

hand-jams 83, 84
hand swap 35
harnesses 38
headpoint 137
heel hooking 119
helmets 39
hexes 30, 147
hierarchy of runners 30
hydration 216

I

IDEAS principles 18
imagery 160–162, 174
independent 18
Istvan Balyi, Dr 207

J

jamming 80, 81
John Bachar 175
John 'Vermin' Sherman 117

K

karabiners 144
kinaesthesia 65, 121, 122
knee-bars 121
Kurt Albert 127

L

lactic acid 91
larks foot 52

layback, the 106, 107
lazy climbing 10, 91, 139, 169
lead climbing 44, 45, 47, 139, 154
learning curve 11
leg loops 38
lock off 35
lock-offs 190
long term development 209
lower-off 35
lunging 124, 197

M

maillon 49
Malcolm Smith 187
mantelshelf, the 108–110
Mark Twight 168
matching 71
mental rehearsal 165
metabolism 181
micro wires 146
mind games 159
mind map 179
Moon board 187
multi-axled cams 147
multi-pitch 48
muscle memory 12

N

nuts 145

O

OBLA level 182, 199, 203
off belay 47
off-hands jams 82
off-width jams 85, 86
one-footed rest 97
on-sight 136
Oscar Eckenstein 117
over cammed 33
overhangs 115, 116
overlap, nuts 29
overloading (training) 183

P

peak height velocity 207, 208
pegs 31
performance profiling 176
periodisation 184
persuasion 166
phosphate 181
phosphocreatine 181, 182
pike 193
pinches 79, 80
placing gear 153, 154

power 196
process vs outcome goals 179
proprioception 13, 65
pull up bars 189
pump, the 58, 91, 185, 199, 203

Q

quickdraws 149, 150, 151, 158

R

rack 143, 144
racks 152
reading routes 134–136
recruitment training 195, 196
redpoint 137
redpointing 127–129
relaxation 171, 172, 174
resting 91
retrievable abseil 50
rigging rope 23
ring-locks 82
ritual, climbing 173
rock-overs 99–101
rocks 145
rock shoes 40
Roland Pauligk 146
roofs 113, 114
rotpunkt 128
RPs 146
rule of opposites, the 102–104

S

safe 47
School Room, the 187
screwgate karabiners 144
scripts, imagery 162, 164
seating a nut 29
second 44
self efficacy 159
self talk 167, 168, 174
sequencing 184
sewing machine leg 194
shake out 91
sidepull 87, 88
single vs double ropes 155
slack 46
slider nuts 146
slopers 79
slow twitch muscle fibres 182
SMART goals 178
smearing, feet 68, 79
solid 20
spikes 30, 31

spotting 53, 54
sprags 79, 80
stacked jams 86
static vs dynamic 123
strength 185
stretching 60–64
style of ascent 136, 137
swapping, feet 71, 72
systems training 187

T

take 46
take in 35
taping up, fingers 78
tat 49
that's me 47
threads 30
Todd Skinner 43
toe hooking 119
top roping 16, 58
trees 32
tri-cams 30
twist-lock 189
typewriter 189

U

undercut 87, 88

V

visualisation 165, 166
VO2 max 181, 203, 204

W

warm up 57–60
watch me 46
weakest link 176
wire gate karabiners 144
wires 145
Wolfgang Güllich 175, 187

Y

Yosemite glove 84
yo-yo 136

Z

zone, the 172